3/8

D1492730

WORKING MEN'S COLLEGE.

LIBRARY REGULATIONS.

The Library is open every week-day evening (except Saturday), from 6.30 to 10 o'clock.

This book may be kept for three weeks. If not returned within that period, the borrower will be liable to a fine of one penny per week.

If lost or damaged, the borrower will be required to make good such loss or damage.

Only one book may be borrowed at a time.

WORKING
COLLEGE
LIBRARY

C. B. Fry at the turn of the century, a great all-rounder.

26607

C. B. FRY

by

DENZIL BATCHELOR

With four plates

WORKING MEN'S COLLEGE LIBRARY

PHOENIX HOUSE LIMITED

LONDON

*To my nephew, Eric Schurmann,
in the hope that I shall one day watch
him against Harrow at Lord's*

This book is copyright in all countries signatory to the Berne
Convention. It may not be reproduced whole or in part by
any method without written permission. Application should
be made in the first place to Phoenix House

Made 1951 in Great Britain
Printed by Butler & Tanner Ltd., Frome and London
for
PHOENIX HOUSE LIMITED
38 William IV Street, London
First published in Great Britain 1951

CONTENTS

CRICKETING LIVES

Short biographies of the heroes of cricket written by their hero-worshippers, intended not only for the enthusiast but for the general reader who is interested in the wedding of English sport and good writing

FIRST TITLES

ILLUSTRATIONS

CHAPTER 1

Magnifico on Olympus

IT IS half-past ten: time for the caravan to start from Brown's Hotel. The Bentley is at the door; Mr. Brooks, the chauffeur, is wise-cracking out of the side of his guttapercha mouth. Aboard are writing pads and binoculars and travelling rugs, a copy of Herodotus, a box of Henry Clay cigars, and reserve hampers of hock and chicken sandwiches in case there has been a strike of caterers in North-West London. A monocle glitters. A silver crest passes, high and haughty, above the cities of the plain. C. B. Fry is off to Lord's.

When the car is held up by the queue milling round the W.G. Gates, a greeting comes through the open window. It is uttered by a thin grey Colonel with the neatly folded look Soames Forsyte wore before he grew up to be imperious and hectoring like Errol Flynn. 'Excuse me, sir, but aren't you C. B. Fry?' It is probably the only time in his life the Colonel has ever spoken to a complete stranger. He does not blush, but he grows a richer grey with sheer embarrassment.

Charles Fry holds up a benevolent forefinger. 'I know exactly what you're going to tell me. You saw me bat in 1909 at Southampton. I made two.'

These shock tactics rattle the Colonel, who has expected nothing more than a little harmless long-distance trench warfare. 'As a matter of fact it *was* Southampton in 1909. But you only made one.'

By rights that should round off the campaign, but it doesn't. The Colonel is taken aboard and transported to Charles's box. Here he sits, day after day. At twelve he is given the cocktail a visitor from Mars has introduced into the box: a straightforward tumbler filled with equal measures of gin and whisky which as soon as it has been christened a Bamboo-shoot is somehow accepted by the company as innocent to the point of being non-alcoholic. He eats lobsters for lunch with that fine Traminer '26, and has strawberries for tea and hears Charles Fry declaim (but not translate) Herodotus, and meets, perhaps, E. V. Lucas, Dr. Dalton, Sir Pelham Warner, Clifford and Arnold Bax, Peggy Ashcroft, Agate and a lady dressed in bridal white from veil to shoe-buckle to celebrate her divorce which becomes absolute during the lunch interval.

Moreover, sometime in the afternoon, another lady whom the host calls My Madam, pays a call. In youth Mrs. Fry was an honorary whip with the Duke of Beaufort's Hounds, and the model for a G. F. Watts' painting: an unusual double. When Charles was a selector of England teams she gave him the benefit of her valued advice. Sometimes she had not actually seen the players in action, but she appeared to have an instinct about their very names which reacted no less sensitively than a dowser's twig. She does not show up for lunch, preferring to eat her sandwiches in the stand, but one feels that when she arrives the cricketers had better pull themselves together. If they don't, some telepathically conveyed barbed paragraph will spring up in the genial flow of Charles's report for the *Evening Standard*.

For while the small talk sparkles, glittering and undangerous as indoor fireworks, and everyone with a nodding acquaintance comes to call, Charles in tussore coat, wide grey felt hat and monocle, continues his effortless production of paragraphs for the column called *C. B. Fry Says*. He writes in staccato style, bringing the picture of the gracious battlefield at Lord's sharply before the reader's eye. He seeks to dramatize the scene, or to offer it to the reader as a film script, not forgetting that, until he tells them, most of his readers have no idea whether or not Paynter is a giant with a cavalry moustache, or that O'Reilly's right arm coils up like a cobra as the snake-charmer calls the tune. He says that he is writing for nursemaids in Wimbledon; for in those days there are nursemaids in Wimbledon. To make quite sure that these ladies are being properly catered for, he occasionally appeals for the veto or imprimatur of the Colonel, sitting in helpless hypnosis at the back of the box. And so the day wears on.

Late in the afternoon it is remembered that an old Wadham friend, now a Colonial Bishop, is believed to be in the President's box. Mr. Brooks is sent off to fetch him for a Bamboo-shoot or a cup of china tea. You see the two of them ambling along past the little mound below the Press Box, where Neville Cardus is generally to be found. Mr. Brooks is in full spate. 'Of course you understand, sir, I don't only drive the Commander, I also do a turn now and then on the Halls. *Public Enemy Number One*—that's the way I'm billed, see. Well, the other night, on I come, dressed up like a Boy Scoutmaster, but still wearing my dog-collar, see. Now this is the point, if you get me, and mark you this story's clean, dead clean, and yet you know you've got to laugh, quite as much as the yarns you really do laugh at when there's only you and the missus. Well, in I come, see, innocent as a babe that's only a twinkle in his father's eye. But what I *don't* know, see, is that this isn't no jamboree at all, it's the Annual General Meeting of Birth Control for Central Africa, see, and the lady in the chair says . . .'

The Bishop waves away the weak tea and opts for the Bamboo-shoot.

That is Charles Fry's box in the great days of old. It will never be the same again. The war wafted Mr. Brooks into industry, and for all I know the Bentley was melted down into a tank, and Charles is no longer a mere Commander, but a Captain, R.N.V.R., and James Agate is dead, having dined with me a night or two before the end, and told me that his final regret was that God would not allow him to last long enough to see the Third World War in which mankind would destroy itself—at the sight of which God would laugh himself to death.

And Madam is dead too. I went down to her memorial service, and Charles wrung me by the hand and said, to hide his emotion, 'Look, I'll show you an infallible way to play a googly.' He had picked up a cricket bat and was demonstrating imperiously, when the chapel bell rang. 'Never mind. We'll finish afterwards.' At which moment, I was reminded of the perfect letter of sympathy, sent by Alexander Woollcott to a bereaved friend: '*Dear Otis, You lucky bum. You had forty years with that delightful woman. How I envy you. Yours sincerely . . .*'

Yes, it was all a long time ago, when the grey Colonel, with his features neatly folded like the features of Soames Forsyte, sat at the back of the box during the four days of a Test Match without anyone discovering his name. You see, if not the Colonel, someone exactly like his unidentified self was always there, in Charles's box at every big game. If not the grey Colonel, a pink clergyman who had strayed out of the very heart of *The Private Secretary*. If not the clergyman, a very old gentleman indeed, who had just returned from Africa, whither he had buried himself in '79, who asked innocently half-way through the third day whether his host had ever taken an active part in cricket himself.

There were years, of course, when there were no boxes to be had. On one midsummer day during one of these, I had a rather bored lady in tow when I ran into Charles. He thought of a way of mellowing this gelid Diana, who only uncurled a nostril when he unbosomed himself of the view that polo was the best of all possible games because the ponies did the work while the men got the applause. He sent a page (I do not know whether M.C.C. has pages on its strength—but he sent a page)—to the Langham at which he had dined on the previous night to fetch a bottle of Liebfraumilch of a vintage which he considered might be worthy of the occasion. The boy (who undoubtedly went both ways on a 53 'bus) was given strict instructions to drive back in a taxi which never exceeded fifteen miles an hour, even if it travelled all the way in second gear. The lady drank the great wine with an air of condescension. She said she had always liked Alsatian wines and could not understand why all her friends affected to despise them.

Then there were the jovial nights, when stumps were drawn and it could be forgotten that Billy Brown, with no strokes at all to which MacLaren would have given august approval, had made a utility double century that would stand in the record book for ever, and be forgotten before the next Test Match. The nights were the signal for white tie and tails, and dancing from ten o'clock till three in the morning. For Charles might (and did) say that polo was probably a better game than cricket, and that Rugby was a better game than soccer, but the one opinion he stood fast on was that the beginning and the end of all the games he respected was dancing. The Greeks knew the secret. A game was not worth the trouble it put you to, unless it was first and last a physical fine art. Cricket was a dance with a bat in your hand, or with the encumbrance of a

10

ball. What was exquisite and memorable was the lyric movement of the artist in action. What was incidental was the score that resulted from his having a bat in his hands, or the analysis that came about from his handling of the ball.

In the dance itself there were no such ignoble impedimenta. The art was pure, not applied. On with the white tie and tails, and let the evening be given over to abandonment to the graces of movement! To surrender oneself to this delight was the surest cure for self-consciousness, which Charles Fry saw as a national failing. Watch the young Englishman enter the ballroom. His hand goes inevitably to his Adam's apple to straighten his tie. When he learns *not* to do that he is at least on the way to the rhythmic control of his body which is the fundamental necessity for success in every game.

Make no mistake about it, Charles Fry has pondered the reason for his pre-eminence as an all-round sportsman. At the end of all his ruminations on the subject, he has no doubt whatsoever that if a man will consent to become an expert dancer first, all these accomplishments shall be added unto him. And almost as a matter of course.

WORKING MEN'S
COLLEGE
LIBRARY

CHAPTER 2

The Nonpareil County Cricketer

HIS OWN story, that leads to the box at Lord's and beyond it, may be said to have begun when as a very small boy he first heard in his Orpington home the voluptuous music of bat against ball in the next-door garden. The two young men there soon invited him to join them at practice, and before long he was playing in his first match of all on the common, and helping to save the game by upholding the last wicket with his own score standing at 17 not out.

Neither in those early days, nor at Repton, nor ever after did he receive any substantial benefit from coaching. There was a weatherbeaten old pro at Repton who used to trundle at nets while uttering the monotonous cry of 'Come forward to it, sir,' whatever the boys did to his bowling. There were an alleged ex-Cambridge twelfth man and an alleged ex-Oxford twelfth man among the masters who occasionally watched the nets and predicted that there was a young batsman who would never make any runs in good-class cricket.

Yet it was at Repton that the foundations of one of the greatest careers in cricket were well and truly laid. It is true that everyone with a claim to omniscience will always tell you (and not without grounds, as we shall see) that Fry learned his cricket from Ranjitsinhji; or (quite unwarrantably) from hours of practice in front of his bedroom mirror. If, however, you ever discuss the matter with Charles himself, or do him the honour of consulting *Life Worth Living*, the autobiography into which he has put his every distilled opinion, you will find that he consistently holds an opposite view today. 'I evolved such cricket as I achieved,' he states, 'by watching Lionel Palairet play and from my own inner nature.' And of the two influences Palairet is entitled to the lesser credit, for the great Somerset batsman was by nature 'a modulated lunger' while Charles himself was a full-swinging driver.

Indeed, it is hard to understand the drift of those who try to see in Fry the defined shadow of the magically insubstantial Ranji. The Jam Sahib, though also a superb driver, was primarily an Eastern conjuror among deflectors of good balls east-by-south-east or west-by-south-west of the wicket-keeper. Charles Fry was the classic example incarnate of the secondary position in batsmanship. Like the proconsular MacLaren, he drew himself up to his full height and raised his bat high behind him when the bowler reared up at the opposite wicket. He was the great puncher past square leg and the great on-driver: over and above his statesmanlike patience in defence. He had the makings of a dominating batsman by the time he was captaining Oxford and scoring his century against Cambridge after being left 16 runs short when the last man came in, with paper-white face, to ground his bat in the block-hole for a whole selfless over.

After the four years in the Oxford team all that was needed to make the Oxford player into a great player was seasoning. This was gained during a tour of South Africa under Lord Hawke's captaincy in the year of the Jamieson Raid. Charles was the most successful batsman in the team. After he had top-scored in many of the early games and drawn away from his rivals by the first Test, Sammy Woods slapped him on the back and said confidentially, 'Charles, I shouldn't be surprised if you and I don't make more runs than all these *good* bats put together.' In fact, Charles finished top of the batting averages, above the great Tom Hayward, and averaged fourteen runs an innings more than Sammy, for whose kindly condescension he was none the less grateful.

You will appreciate how much that tour did for him when you look at his subsequent record. At first he had few opportunities of first-class cricket, but a season or two later he had all the scope he needed. For three summers around the turn of the century he and Ranjitsinhji hardly knew the meaning of failure. In 1901, both were at their absolute peak. Charles scored 3,147 runs, heading the first-class batting with an average of 78·67, while Ranji came fairly close on his heels, having hit nearly 2,500 runs for an average of over 70.

If Charles had had the chance of playing regularly in May, the record-breakers might be filling the headlines of the second half of the twentieth century by their efforts to eclipse his season's crop of 4,000. But he began with an injury and scored barely a hundred runs in the first month.

He finished that summer in a full crescendo of triumph. Between August 16th and the end of the season he scored six consecutive centuries in first-class cricket; a record which after all these years even Don Bradman has only equalled. Moreover, for the record, Bradman got his string of centuries on pluperfect Australian wickets while Charles's runs against Hampshire (with South Africa's Llewellyn to harass him) and Surrey (with "Razor" Smith, Lees and Tom Hayward on the strength) were both achieved on rain-damaged pitches—really nasty wickets on which Don would have been grateful for double figures.

In those days the world knew Charles Fry as essentially an on-side player. He rarely cut and seldom off-drove; but in execution of the leg-hit that made square leg duck instinctively, of the full-blooded pull, and of the majestic on-drive he had few peers among the batsmen of the Golden Age. Mark well—I say the batsmen; but I think Charles would hold the opinion that I was overlooking the serious consideration to which he was entitled as a fast bowler. He was the type of fast bowler J. M. Barrie dreamed of being; and he was good enough to get two hat-tricks at Lord's, to take 6 for 78 in his last 'Varsity Match, and to be picked for the Gentlemen as an opening bowler.

In the end, Jim Phillips, the strong-arm umpire from Australia, mastered him as the batsmen of the day never could. He no-balled him on the grounds of stern disapproval of his action. Jim Phillips was a pioneer in the veto worth his place in the Russian team. He had blazed the trail by no-balling Jones during Stoddart's second tour in Australia—if he hadn't had the strength of mind to do that, it was the opinion of Sydney Pardon that the cry of no-ball would never have been raised against throwers in this country. Then he came to England with an ambition to figure as a mining-engineer buzzing in his brain-box, and a copy of Hall and Knight's algebra ostentatiously protruding from the pocket of his umpire's white coat. His most remarkable achievement in these islands was to no-ball Mold sixteen times in ten overs at Old Trafford in '96, when Lancashire were playing Somerset. Having created the sensation of the season, he folded his arms and assumed a mask of disinterest while Mold bowled unchanged through the second innings. There was fervent support for the bowler, whose friends did not fail to point out that such a thing had never happened to him before during his dozen seasons in first-class cricket. Nobody bothered to point out that six years earlier his action had been condemned as unfair by a majority of eleven to one at a meeting of county captains. Charles Fry was the third great figure to be denounced by Phillips. His retort was what was to be expected of him. When he came out in the second innings his right arm was encased in a splint with the sleeve carefully buttoned over it at the wrist. This ought to have proved the matter one way or another for ever: but W. L. Murdoch, the Sussex captain, was not prepared to allow the experiment to take place. It was hard luck to have one's career as a fast bowler blasted before its prime; but there was still a bit of batting to be done.

But even though Jim Phillips could do little to impugn his masterfulness here (though as will be seen, he contributed his mite), you will sometimes, to this day, find the knowledge-

14

able talking carpingly behind the back of their hands about Charles's record as a Test Match batsman. Didn't he make some 30,000 runs in first-class cricket with an average of nearly 50? Didn't he score 3,000 in one season (with 13 centuries), and didn't he also hit two centuries in a match no less than five times? This stamps him as about the greatest run-getter in the game during the first dozen years of the twentieth century. Moreover, you couldn't say that he wasn't the man for the big occasion.

It was D. R. Jardine who once acutely observed that the way to assess a batsman was to have a look at his performances against Northern county sides. That was true enough in his time: in Charles's heyday it was probably only necessary to keep your eye on how he fared against Yorkshire. If a man could make runs against Hirst and Rhodes, Haigh, J. T. Brown and F. S. Jackson, he was a national hero.

Do not forget that between the turn of the century and World War I there were plenty of solid citizens glued to their seats in the Long Room who genuinely resented the intruders from Australia. They distracted attention from the main business of cricket, which was to help your side to win the County Championship. A fly-by-night success in the unwholesome, torrid atmosphere engendered by those theatrical Test Matches took the minds of all but the most serious off the natural supremacy open to the cricketer: success in Gentlemen v. Players. That was the attitude adopted by the diehard on the high stool behind the big plate-glass windows, when cavalry regiments still rode horses and the Liberalism of Lloyd George was regarded as naked anarchy.

Well, all through those years Charles Fry was the greatest run-getting machine in cricket; he rose to new heights of supremacy when it came to measuring weapons with the Yorkshire bowlers; and he was unsurpassed in his triumphs against the Players. It was his success in these branches of the game, in the *real* cricket, the sempiternal cricket, that established him as the dominant figure of his generation.

It is sometimes forgotten that he began, before he went up to Oxford, as a Surrey batsman. As far as I remember he did not score many, or any, runs, and (like Philip Mead in later years) he was allowed to leave the Oval by the back door without any very pressing invitation to return. By the mid-nineties he had reached ripeness, and Sussex, not Surrey, was reaping the harvest. He continued in the county side until 1908, after which he emigrated to Hampshire with the mission of keeping T.S. *Mercury* in being and, on the side, of stiffening the Hampshire batting.

His greatest cricket, over the years, was given to Sussex. For season upon season he and K. S. Ranjitsinhji were a pair of names in the batting order more daunting in association than any dreamed of by this generation of bowlers. They were more dreadful than Hobbs and Sutcliffe, or Woodfull and Ponsford, or Compton and Edrich. If one failed, the other was sure to make two hundred: if neither failed, they shared the two hundred between them. In the halcyon summers of the century's first lustre it seemed that neither ever failed. At one end was Fry, with Coeur de Lion's broadsword; at the other, Ranji, like Saladin in *The Talisman* with black magic in his slim wrists which could cut a silk handkerchief in two with a flicker of the scimitar. They made their momentous scores, year after year after year, when defensive batting did not exist: when you played aggressive strokes—each one fraught with real risk—at bowling which was always aggressive too. In those days there was no laying five length balls dead at your feet, and pulling the long-hopping sixth for a single or a boundary. In those days a half-volley was not a serious menace to be circumnavigated as carefully as a Parliamentary question; but a gift to be driven with widened shoulders and whirring bat.

In county cricket Charles was early into his stride. For Sussex he scored more than eighteen hundred of the twenty-three hundred odd runs he made in 1899, and among his centuries there was of course one against Yorkshire. But he reached his peak in 1901. Five times he was to score more than 2,000 runs in a season; but in that immortal season he exceeded 3,000. That summer too, he hit his six centuries in a row.

But there were other great years as well. There was 1903, for example, when even the bewildered *Wisden* had to admit that he overshadowed Ranjitsinhji as a Sussex batsman. And the very next year there he was again, taking part in hardly more than half the innings that the next men on the list, Ranji and Joe Vine, played together; and scoring nearly twice as many

RKING MEN
COLLEGE
LIBRARY

In action:
'He would be better with more patience' *said a critic.*

runs as the two of them. His batting average for Sussex stood at 79, and among his big innings was a double century (229 out of 377) against Yorkshire at Hove, and 177 against Hirst, Rhodes, Haigh and Jackson at Sheffield. With Ranji, he added 255 on that occasion in less than four hours, and had the satisfaction of being gently chided by *Wisden* for being less enterprising than might have been expected.

He maintained his dominion to the very end. In 1908, his last year for Sussex, he played only ten innings, but three of them were centuries.

He was able to give less time to Hampshire cricket than he had given to Sussex; but when he could play, his form was as majestic as ever. He was still there, drawing himself up to his full height, swinging his bat up above the middle stump, and when the intimidated bowler delivered what he feebly hoped might turn out to be a thunderbolt, lashing out with authority so that the straight drives and the on-drives rang against the railings.

These were great occasions for Hampshire too. In 1912, the year of the Triangular Tests, though he finished head of the first-class averages he was only able to bat seven times for the county, but he averaged over a hundred for the team, and one of his centuries was (as usual) hit against Yorkshire.

Even the glimpse the southern cricket fields had of him after World War I (when in his fiftieth year he was still good for big scores) showed a figure of heroic stature to a new generation whose champions were barely stock-size. Those who saw him score his half-century off McDonald and Mailey, as if they too were no more than human, had their eyes dazzled for an hour by the burnish on the grand manner that had come out of the Golden Age.

Such were the high deeds and heroic feats of the champion county cricketer between the time of the Boer War and the outbreak of the Kaiser's War.

Well then, why were his Test Match scores very much less impressive? In 29 innings against Australia he made 825 runs, with one century in 1905, and an average of 31. What was there about Test Matches that brought him down a peg or two?

There are, I think, two things to be said on this subject. The first is that Charles's Test Match record compares well with those of the giants of his time, though it may be statistically dwarfed by the achievements of today's defensive batsmen against mediocre bowling on lifeless wickets. That average of 31 is higher than that of J. T. Tyldesley for instance, or that of Braund, or M. A. Noble, or Syd Gregory. If you measure sheer lyricism or the major artistic glories by the yardstick of 'those damned dots', Charles Fry's Test Match average is one run an innings below that of that mediocre run-getter, Victor Trumper. Surely you would be a bold man to assume that any of your half-dozen current heroes with averages twice as inflated was a more valuable batsman than Trumper?

That is the first point to be made for the defence; though, indeed, in this matter, I am sure Charles Fry would disdain to enter the box for cross-examination. Like that other regal Charles, he would hold his anointed head in the air and refuse his judges.

The second point is that, whether or not because he was never good at registering a becoming meekness in the face of authority, Charles found himself out of England teams on numerous occasions when he should have been padded-up as the hope of his side.

WORKING MEN'S
COLLEGE
LIBRARY

CHAPTER 3

The Intermittent Test Player

IF YOU follow him through his Test Match career, you will see what I mean. After his impressive debut in South Africa, he played in all five matches against Australia in '99. He was top scorer in his first innings, and did well at Leeds and in the Oval game. He had, you may say, established an inalienable right to a place in the side. But the next set of Tests was in Australia, and Charles happened to be that now obsolete phenomenon, an amateur with his living to earn. He was at this time writing articles for the *Athletic News* and the *Express*, the *Daily Chronicle*, the *Captain* and the *Strand*. He couldn't afford the time to take part in the series of defeats sustained by MacLaren's less than representative team.

Before the year was over the Australians were with us again; and those games of the summer of 1902 were probably the greatest and most absorbing of the whole series. It is commonly claimed that the side England put into the field at Birmingham for the first match was the best ever picked. Here it is, in its batting order: A. C. MacLaren, C. B. Fry, K. S. Ranjitsinhji, F. S. Jackson, Tyldesley, Lilley, Hirst, G. L. Jessop, Braund, Lockwood and Rhodes. In the game, Charles was caught at the wicket off the fast bowler for a duck, and Ranji and MacLaren were back in the pavilion before 40 was on the board, but the side went on to declare with 376 for 9 wickets. Then, after a night of rain, Hirst (much the more dangerous bowler) took three wickets, and the comparatively innocuous Rhodes took seven, and the Australians were put out for 36. They followed on, lost two wickets for 46; and then the rain saved them.

The game at Lord's was also flooded out. Once again Charles did not score. He was snapped up off a leg glance by Clem Hill, who was moved across from slip to square leg, and happened to be in the right place at the right split-second. Never was there a better example of a rolling stone gathering a valuable helping of moss.

The third game at Sheffield was Charles's last appearance in the series. He was one of eight batting failures in the side. They dropped him for the Fourth Test, replacing him with Bobby Abel, very much less effective on a wet wicket. Perhaps, as the game was at Manchester, the selectors confidently looked for a bone-dry pitch. They certainly behaved as if they were quite as much out of their minds as that. They failed to pick Haigh, because Lord Hawke would not allow the Yorkshire player leave of absence to play for England.

Even so, it was hard to be out of the two greatest finishes in the whole history of England-Australia matches. The first was a defeat by 3 runs—when Fred Tate dropped Darling off a skier, and was bowled off-stump after waiting for three-quarters of an hour for the rain to stop so that he could bustle for the one boundary needed for victory. The second was the Oval game, in which Jessop hit his dazzling century, and Hirst and Rhodes made 14 runs wanted in a last-wicket partnership whose temperature never rose above normal.

It was hard, too, to be unavailable for the team which sailed to retrieve the Ashes in the following winter. But by 1904 Charles was embarking on the editorship of *C. B. Fry's Magazine*. He was busy rounding up contributions from little-known aspirants like P. G. Wodehouse, or keeping E. V. Lucas up to the mark as an author of articles on cricket, or himself writing the first article in English journalism on the conquest of the air, or helping M. Georges Phillipart to launch a new game he had invented, which Charles amused himself by christening 'Diabolo'.

So there were no Tests for him from the first week of July, 1902, till the last week of May, 1905. Don't forget, too, that in the wet summer of 1903 he proved himself easily the greatest run-gatherer in the country. Mainly by off-strokes and those straight drives which few people credited him with possessing, he scored five hundred runs more than his nearest rival, Tom Hayward, besides boasting an average of over 81 while Tom's was anchored down to 35.

There were great hopes that 1905 would be a dazzling year for this Forgotten Man of the Tests. He had averaged 70 for his 2,800 runs in the previous summer; and indeed, only in that sad season of 1902, had he failed to be a glutton for runs.

Those high hopes for 1905 were amply fulfilled. He missed the First Test, handsomely won at Nottingham, as a result of seriously injuring a thumb while batting to the bowling of a tot in short pants, on his home ground. But his 73 was the best knock in the English first innings at Lord's. He was sweeping forward under a full press of sail towards his century, when that same Jim Phillips, who years before had disqualified his fast bowling, interpreted a ball that bounced off the toe of his boot as a palpable catch at the wicket.

But the season's best game for Charles was the final drawn match at the Oval. In it he scored his only Test Match century against Australia. This flawless 144 glittered with marvellous off-drives and superb cuts. The Australian theory that he was an easy batsman to damp down provided you cut off his blaze of strokes on the on-side was totally disproved.

The next Test tour was to South Africa: and the team lost

four of its five Test Matches without benefit of his assistance. But in spite of a ruptured Achilles tendon he was on deck in May 1906, when the immensely strong South African team arrived in the following summer. This was a great side, which so impregnated England with the doctrine of the googly that the strain persists today, in spite of the fact that the conjuring trick can now expect to find itself solved by simple-minded tail-enders. The particular geniuses of the South African attack were R. O. Schwarz, the widest-breaking googler in history, who could not spin the ball from leg; A. E. Vogler, who added swerving, medium-paced bowling to his slow-medium googlies; and Aubrey Faulkner, the most deceptive purveyor of mystery balls in the side. There was also a superb fast bowler in J. J. Kotze.

The Second Test at Leeds was one of the most remarkable big games ever fought out in England. It was played on a classic glue-pot from start to finish, and Faulkner helped himself to 6 wickets for 17 runs while England scratched a pitiful 76 in the first innings. Only Hayward, Hirst and J. T. Tyldesley reached double figures on that Jack-in-a-box of a wicket. It was after the lunch interval on the first day that the pitch developed its full diabolism, when 9 English wickets fell for 42 runs.

Then it was England's turn. The pitch, though slightly less treacherous, was made for Blythe, and he took advantage of every gremlin lurking on the premises. Sherwell and Shalders struck out defiantly, and not without luck. They helped their side to a useful lead of 34 runs. England made 162 in the second innings; Charles's 54 against superb bowling on a wicket which gave the attack great assistance, being an innings of heroic dimensions. It was also a match-winning effort; begun when three-quarters of an hour's play remained on the second day, and R. E. Foster, the England captain, had to be argued out of a plan to turn his batting order upside down. Blythe bowled as marvellously as ever in the second innings, though the effort of taking fifteen wickets in the match without sending down a single bad ball, brought about an epileptic fit. The match was won; but if Charles had made a duck in the second innings, South Africa would have scraped home victorious by one run.

The final Test at the Oval was drawn, brought to a premature end on the third day by bad light. The game would surely have been lost, and the rubber only squared, if Charles had not played what he has always regarded as the finest innings of his life. His 144 was made on a wicket which might have been hand-tailored for the bowlers, who made the very most of their chances.

When the critics make up carping minds that C. B. Fry, though the dominie in county cricket, was strangely unimposing in international games, they would do well to recall this rarely remembered rubber against one of the strongest teams that ever visited England. In the two crucial matches, the subject of their agnosticism was the one batsman who came to the rescue of a sorely harassed side: with Colin Blythe's help, he made a victorious summer of what would otherwise have been a very lean season indeed.

Many necessary names were missing from the team A. O. Jones took to Australia at the end of that season. There was no MacLaren, no Spooner or Jessop or J. T. Tyldesley or George Hirst: and of course, as usual, there was no Charles Fry. By 1908 he had become involved in running Training Ship *Mercury*, where within two years he was to help increase the number of boys passing out into the Navy in the Advanced Class from five to fifty-five. This sort of work must have been some consolation for absence from an England team which lost four out of five Tests.

In 1909, the Australians were back, and Archie MacLaren was captaining England for the last time. Charles played in the first, third and fifth games, but was at his majestic best only in the last match when run out for 62, as a result of Wilfred Rhodes at first deciding that a genteel pat to mid-off was worth a single and afterwards silently rescinding this unbalanced decision.

Following that summer of 1909 came two rubbers of Test Matches upon which the light of Charles's countenance never shone. England lost to South Africa in 1909–10, and won in Australia the following winter.

To sum up: from 1899 till the end of the Australian season of 1911–12, there had been no year when Charles was not, on his merits, entitled to a place, and a place of honour, in the

England side. Yet, for one reason and another, he played in only fifteen of the forty-five Tests fought out during this period.

WORKING MEN'S
COLLEGE
LIBRARY

CHAPTER 4

Triangular Tournament: at the Apex

IT WAS as well that in 1912, virtually at the end of his career as a first-class cricketer, the Triangular Tests gave him his final opportunity to stamp his personality on the international game.

It cannot be said that this opportunity was made available very gracefully. For the first time in history the authorities at Lord's made an offer of the England captaincy, not for the whole series, but for the First Test only. Charles treated this offer with the urbane disdain it merited; and, as a result, found himself voted the plenipotentiary powers he needed, qualified only by the setting up of a Selection Committee which met once at the beginning of the season, picked a team, and then broke up for the summer.

The team it picked was good enough to overwhelm South Africa and to win decisively in the only Test brought to a conclusion against Australia. As it happened, it wasn't a hard task. South Africa was unrecognizably weak when compared with the great team of five years earlier. Faulkner, ill in May, never seemed to recover the confidence necessary to dominate the batting order. Nourse was the only batsman who showed any consistency in the Tests, and his form would hardly have gained him a place in either of the other two sides.

But the pitiful failure of the bowling was the main reason for the side's ineffectual performances in the big games. Faulkner was much less dangerous than he had been in the past, and Schwarz was hardly dangerous at all. There was no fast bowler in the side, and the only man who gave the attack any distinction was a newcomer in S. J. Pegler, a medium-pace bowler with a sharp leg-break, who could very occasionally turn the ball the other way and who never allowed his length

23

to get ragged however severely fate treated him. He took more Test Match wickets than all the rest of the team's bowlers put together; and at the end of the tour his captain, Frank Mitchell, publicly made it known that in his opinion the future of South African cricket depended on the coming generation mastering his technique rather than that of the bowlers of the googly who had first raised the country to parity with England and Australia. Pegler was to continue in international cricket for fifteen years, but he was never again to be as formidable as against England at Lord's or Australia at Nottingham in that abominable summer of 1912. He was born at the wrong time. If he had been five years older he would have given such variety to Sherwell's touring team as would have made it downright invincible.

If the South Africans were disappointingly weak, the Australians were also poor; and this because they were very much less than representative. They had been given all the time they demanded to assemble the strongest possible team, and they had spent it in a sort of Civil War between the Board of Control and the leading cricketers. In the end, when the team sailed, five at least of the greatest players were missing—Trumper, Ransford, Armstrong, Clem Hill and Cotter.

Such a travesty of a side was not extraordinarily interesting to English crowds, and the gates they drew were comparatively poor. The batting was far below Australian standards. At forty-two, S. E. Gregory was not the force he had been in the past. Fortunately Bardsley was in immense form, and this solid smiter convinced the critics that he was a sparkling driver and a more energetic lugger of balls to the leg boundary than Clem Hill himself—even then, as now, the yardstick against whom all left-handers must submit to be measured.

Macartney, who had appeared in one Test against Warner's second team, was the other success among the batsmen. He had the footwork of a Pedlar Palmer and the effrontery of a Sicilian bandit. Not even Trumper had been as ready to force balls to the boundary as arrogantly as this Hotspur during those early overs when properly brought-up batsmen are getting their sober eyes in.

After these two, there was, before the back of the batting was broken, only the sombre Kelleway, diligent to the point of

24

dullness, and with a special relish in his misanthropic make-up for the pain he inflicted on spectators of good will. His batting took on an extra coating of dourness whenever a Test Match hove in sight, and his medium-pace bowling was fairly effective on the few batsmen's wickets available.

The Australian bowling was a good deal stronger than the batting. If there was no Cotter, there was a hard worker in Whitty, and a good swerver with a useful nip from the off in Hazlitt, who began the season with an action that would nowadays strain diplomatic relations with the Dominion, but who was later prevailed upon to reform. On the wet wickets that abounded from Edinburgh to Southampton, Macartney was probably the best prospect on the strength; but Gregory was rightly reluctant to take the edge off his Damascene batsmanship by bowling him extensively.

It was not, therefore, an immense task that lay ahead of Charles Fry in the summer of 1912, this winning of the un-challenged supremacy by finishing at the apex of the triangle. All the same, no captain can do more than win the games he finds himself assigned to play: and that Charles set out to do.

The side he got together cannot have been far short of the best ever fielded for England. It could be faulted on two grounds only: it had room for one more really good batsman, and it lacked a fast bowler of blood royal. Walter Brearley bowled six overs in the series, and Hitch appeared in two games without being called upon to bowl. The fact was that with Barnes and Foster, and Woolley and Dean for wet wickets, you could win all the Test Matches needed without anyone noticing your deficiencies in more than an academic way.

This was the batting order for the last of the six games: Hobbs, Rhodes, R. H. Spooner, C. B. Fry, Woolley, Hearne, J. W. H. T. Douglas, F. R. Foster, Smith, Barnes and Dean. Yes, it carried fewer guns than the ironclad of 1902; but I fancy it would have blown most modern elevens to smithereens. Do you think Bradman would have made triple centuries and Ponsford would have finished his career with a Test Match average of nearly fifty if they'd had Barnes and Foster at their throats? I don't.

If I had been captaining the England side (and I am bound

to admit the suggestion never seems to have been seriously considered), my own fear would have been that in a wet summer an early match might have been flukishly lost to Australia. With only three Tests against each enemy such a handicap (again in a wet summer) could hardly have been overcome. But Charles was coolly confident that there need be no apprehension about any such accident.

Australia began by overwhelming South Africa at Manchester in the last week in May; and then England met the losers at Lord's a fortnight later. Frank Mitchell won the toss, and decided to bat on a pitch saturated from the week-end rain which had dried more quickly than anyone anticipated. In twenty-six overs and one ball, Barnes and Foster got rid of the whole side. In the first four overs, Hartigan went to an elegant catch in the slips by Foster, and Herbie Taylor was out l.b.w.—Barnes taking both wickets. Then Nourse and Llewellyn stood their ground and flailed away at the bowling, before Foster knocked the former's wicket askew with a shooter, and then uprooted Taylor's off stump with a magnificent ball. Two for 35 soon became side out for 55. Barnes (though Foster had the better analysis and hit the wicket five times) was the senior partner in accomplishing this pogrom. As Charles said of him on another occasion, the batsmen found him quite unplayable, and if they could have played him they would have made fewer runs.

England began inauspiciously, Hobbs playing-on in the first over. After that, however, the innings was almost as lighthearted as a romp with the children. Spooner and Rhodes dominated the bowling until the end of the day, scoring at the sort of pace rarely seen at Lord's nowadays except when the Players are batting against the Gentlemen. If Pegler had not unleashed a spell not so much of bowling as of black magic, when put on after lunch with the pavilion behind his low-flighted leg-breaks, the score might have bulged over the straining limits of the score-board. As it was, it was respectably massive because of Spooner's graceful assaults on short-pitched leg-breaks and because of an hour and a half of Woolley, luxuriating with flowing drives and effortless leg glides.

The match died in its bed on the third day. Llewellyn, later a gifted all-rounder in the Hampshire side, vigorously drove

Barnes and Foster to the lightly policed boundaries and was not dismayed even when Jack Hobbs was incited by his captain to try his hand as a fast bowler.

If there was anything in the victory by an innings and 62 runs to make the England captain uneasy, it was the team's failure to hold its catches. Pegler was dropped thrice by the time Barnes knocked his wicket down for ten.

A fortnight later came the first match with Australia, also at Lord's. By the simple standards of those days, before television and wireless provided 'gates' of a few million, there was immense public interest in this trial of strength. Unfortunately a promising game was liquidated. There were three hours of cricket on the first day, and less than half an hour on the second. The third day, to show that not only Manchester can rub in the irony of a ruined Test Match was golden enough for a Royal Garden Party. As there didn't happen to be any such thing arranged, Royalty honoured the game with a visit. I do not know whether it was on this occasion that Charles was greeted with, 'Well, I watched you bat; and you certainly played some very good innings.'

The match was chiefly memorable for a handsome century by Jack Hobbs and an even better-looking 99 by Macartney. The English innings (310 for 7 wickets declared) did not come to an end until the morning of the third day; and though this was mainly attributable to the fact that for most of the time there was no play at all, there was some indigestible batting in the brief intervals of alleged activity. Charles tried to inject a feeling of urgency into the proceedings, and ran himself out in a game effort to score two off a defensive stroke to the bowler.

Macartney was the unluckiest and Hazlitt the luckiest player in this game. Everybody who hasn't enjoyed the experience is ready to explain that getting out for 99 is no misfortune—the few who achieve it are certain to be remembered when many who swell the list of century-makers have long been forgotten. But you have to be a good sportsman to enjoy being given out caught wicket at 99, when you have *missed* the leg-glide which would have given you the century that statisticians assure you is so unimportant. As for Hazlitt, his bent-arm action sent waves of apoplexy down the Long Room; which later seethed with indignation at Charles's inexplicable refusal to give the

27

Australians some buckshee batting practice against Woolley, the most formidable wet-wicket bowler in his side.

In July the South Africans were emphatically beaten at Leeds, and the Second Test with Australia was punctually washed out at the Old Trafford. The former game was remarkable for some vintage bowling by Barnes, well supported by Dean of Lancashire who during this season gave up the attempt to imitate George Hirst and increased his stature as a wet-wicket bowler in consequence. There was also some buoyant batting from Hobbs (in Charles's view a different and superior player in the pre-World War I era), and an invaluable defensive masterpiece from R. H. Spooner, unrecognizable as one of those Fragonard decorations usually brushed off by the blade of this Young Master.

As for the Australian Test at Old Trafford, it was reduced to three hours on the first afternoon and an hour on the second day. In the circumstances both sides would have been better off watching Fatty Arbuckle at the local Bioscope, but if Hazlitt at point had not dropped a simple catch from Rhodes before he had scored, Australia might have got England out by the tea-interval on the first day and at least reduced a platitudinous draw to a state of frenzy. As it was, Rhodes continued to bat without lifting a ball from the quagmire till he had made 92 side-saving runs. The rest of the team had a whack and were caught off skiers.

August held the last two matches of the series. In two days, England beat South Africa by 10 wickets at the Oval. This game marked the apotheosis of Sidney Barnes, always assuming that he failed to get himself deified in Melbourne in 1912, when he took 5 of the best Australian wickets for 6 runs off 11 overs, 7 of them maidens. ('No, sir—not Mr. Trumper's. I missed his by the thickness of a sheet of tissue paper,' he once explained to me whilst we watched the floods rising on the Old Trafford Test of '37. 'The secret of it, sir? Well—to tell you the truth, I was bowling . . . rather well.')

On this sombre Monday afternoon, a few months later, he recaptured that invincible mood in which no English bowler, not even Larwood, has inflated his heroic chest since. He smacked down Tancred's wicket at once, shortly afterwards discovered in the funereal pitch enough devilry to send a ball

28

jack-in-the-boxing into Smith's face with so much violence that Spooner had to go through the motions of wicket-keeping while somebody held that Tiger as his beribboned lip was stitched together. Taylor (that master of back play) and Snooke volleyed four death-or-glory boundaries off Barnes, but almost every one of the other twelve runs accrued while he collected his half-dozen wickets came from bats with two edges to them and nothing in between. When it was England's turn, Faulkner beat bat and wicket at least a couple of times an over, and found Hobbs the only opponent worthy of his steel. In less than two hours he scored 68 runs by uninhibited forward strokes and wide-chested pulls off the right foot to the square-leg boundary. When Faulkner was at his most dominating, Hobbs coolly on-drove him for three clinking boundaries in an over. So long as he had Spooner to gleam at the far end like a knight in armour through the gloom over Kennington, there was always a chance of a neat little score for the side, which, by the standards of the season, would loom up as a match-winning total.

As it was, Barnes overwhelmed South Africa more completely in the second than in the first innings. Only Nourse batted as if sentence of death had yet to be passed; and even when he and Faulkner were windmilling away, to the tune of 44 runs in half an hour, every ball looked like being somebody's last. Twice Barnes bowled him morally, as he did everybody else on the side, except Tancred—Woolley's victim before he could fire a shot at him. South African batsmen firmly declared (it was the only firm thing about them on the day's showing), that there had never been such an enemy to contend with as this implacable bowler of quick leg-breaks and sharp break-backs whose length was remorselessly exact. Often during the series, Charles had found that a rheumatic tendency which developed late during a game made Barnes a doubtful factor in the second innings, however fine might be his work on the first day. But for once he kept the best of his superlative self till the second service. There has probably never been better bowling in a Test Match in England than he uncorked, in all its bubbling glory, in the second innings of this match.

And so to the final game, the Third and last Test Match against Syd Gregory's Australians. Both England and Australia being unbeaten, and the South Africans having lost five and drawn one of their matches, it was decided that the winner of this game was to take rank as the overall winner of the series. Moreover, time being no object, and there being for once not so much as a shadow of a war on the horizon, it was further decided that this game was to be played to a finish.

So here it was, the match of matches, upon which the supremacy in the world of cricket was to be determined; upon which Charles Fry's reputation as an incomparable captain was to be staked.

The battle began long before the cricket. Before a ball was bowled, there was such another chess-game as was to be played in years to come between Bradman and Allen—the two captains jockeying each other's teams into occupation of the Melbourne middle while the sun boiled the puddly wicket to glue. This Test of 1912 was slated to begin on the Monday morning after a week-end of downpour. A crowd of 30,000 sat in Monday's sun and read the earlier editions of the evening papers which explained to the meanest intelligence why Fry was the sort of meek-eyed captain who was bound to be put upon and trampled to pieces by the wily Australians.

The sun shone—but there was no cricket. The crowd grew restless. They could not see from their seats around the boundary the black sponge that was the wicket. The Surrey authorities were perturbed at the volcanic atmosphere; and up came Syd Gregory, whose only motive in life appeared to be to keep the spectators happy, to suggest that they should toss for choice of innings, and get on with the game. But Charles did not quite see it that way. The only chance Gregory had of winning this game was of winning the toss and putting England in on a wicket unfit for human consumption. His cry of 'Duckie, duckie, duckie, come and be killed' fell on deaf ears. Charles would not start the game until there was a cricket pitch to play it on.

Late in the afternoon, this condition being fulfilled, he won the toss, and took first innings. After Hobbs had been caught at the wicket for a brilliant 66, and Spooner had been marvellously taken left-handed by Hazlitt at short leg inches off the grass, the captain whose firmness had given England an honest chance of winning the crucial Test Match was booed as he walked to the wicket. Democracy had found out that he was the captain who objected to mud-larking, and democracy didn't see why it should not have its money's worth, whatever the state of the wicket.

The English first innings, after Hobbs had left his elegant hall-mark on it, was saved by the brilliance of Woolley and the dogged Yorkshire suspiciousness with which Rhodes held the bowling at arm's length while acquiring 49 resourceful runs.

Next day there was an hour and a half's play between a night of waterspout and an evening of floods. In between, England were bustled out for the moderate score of 245, and Australia put 51 runs on the board at the cost of the two valuable wickets of Gregory and Macartney.

The third day too was better suited to water polo than to cricket. Kelleway and Bardsley jogged along without apparent discomfort, playing back with discretion and taking singles whenever the ball bounced short. They took the score to 90, when disaster overtook them. Woolley somehow penetrated the iron curtain of Kelleway's defence and hit a vulnerable pad. Bardsley was out to a ball from Barnes which pitched so wide to the on that he disdained to aim a stroke at it, and then saw himself bowled behind his mortified legs.

The Gadarene herd could not have plunged to destruction faster than the remainder of the Australian batsmen. Ninety for two soon became 111 for 10 wickets. Charles's refusal to unmask Woolley against the Australians at Lord's was justified in full measure. No one could shape a stroke at him on this rain-damaged wicket.

A lead of 134 looked decisive in a match of this type; but the beginning of England's second innings in Stygian gloom after the lunch interval was enough to daunt any but the stoutest-hearted captain. With seven on the board, Whitty bowled Rhodes all over his wicket, and the very next ball Spooner guided into the palms of Jennings at slips. Another dozen such overs, and England must have been deep in the danger zone. But the black skies cracked, and when the rain ceased at tea-time many of the devils in the pitch were waterlogged or drowned.

Nevertheless the bowling was keen, the outfield unhelpful: and for eight overs there was only one scoring stroke, and that was unintentional. But the batsmen persisted. Hobbs pulled anything short of a length with zeal. Fry's defence was as august as Kelleway's, and every now and then he picked the ball that could be hit and swung with the blade behind the hands until after the moment of impact. Elbow and shoulder pointed in the direction the ball was driven: the left foot was advanced close to the line of the ball. An innings of cardinal importance was being built up over after over, while Hobbs was brilliantly snapped up by Matthews at point, and five runs later Woolley heard his wickets shattered by a fine swerving off-break from Hazlitt. Rain and darkness fell, and appeals went up against the twilight; but still Charles Fry kept the bowling at bay.

Next morning he carried on the good work. He lost Hearne after a few overs of brisk aggression, and there was a moment when, if D. Smith had not been stranded flat-footed at square leg, he might have found pounce enough to cut him off in his prime. But there was not a chance that came to hand; not a moment when the most chicken-hearted had a right to feel apprehensive, till, with a lead of over 300 on the board, he played a stroke that raised a chunk of turf as well as a less than firmly hit drive to Jennings. Hazlitt then folded up the rest of the side as unconcernedly as if it had been a pair of white flannel trousers.

Australia's second innings opened in an atmosphere of high drama. After Barnes had bowled one over, Kelleway carved a firm stroke from Dean south of backward point. J. W. H. T. Douglas flung a hand out: the ball stuck: became unstuck: was tickled by his fingertips, skidded shyly away; was clutched: oozed out of his palms—and was finally pouched after an exhibition fit for a Command Performance. Macartney then joined Jennings, and the Command Performance suddenly became a harlequinade. Barnes was hit round the corner for two sterling boundaries by Jennings; and Macartney sabred and slashed and bastinadoed first Barnes and then Woolley as if he had the most sober intentions of getting the 300 or so needed for victory between the tea-interval and close of play.

The sunburst was too good to last. Quickly came the deluge. At 46, Jennings hit Woolley higher than the Tower of Babel beyond cover. The voice of Fry called on Rhodes and Smith the wicket-keeper, and George Hirst (who hadn't been in the

WORKING MEN'S
COLLEGE
LIBRARY

Gentlemen v. Players, Lord's, 1899.

L–R. Back row: umpire, W. M. Bradley, A. C. MacLaren, C. L. Townsend, umpire. Middle row: G. MacGregor,
K. S. Ranjitsinhji, W. G. Grace, R. M. P... F... N. S. A...

English side that summer) to consummate the catch: then he darted forward himself from silly point to take the ball ankle-high with one hand.

A few balls later Dean bowled down Macartney's defiant wicket. Then Bardsley, ambling a cosy single, was thrown out by the puma-like Hobbs from cover—to the astonishment of several players and many occupants of the Long Room with their faces turned to the bar. After that Australia never rallied. Woolley caught and bowled Matthews, took Hazlitt's wicket, and clean bowled Whitty. Half an hour after the game ended the rain teemed down, to last for the next two days. As this first 'timeless Test' was to last 'a week if necessary' (the absolute outside limit that imagination had considered possible for such a game), Woolley's final spell was needed to win the rubber for England.

But for Charles's refusal to start the game when Gregory tried to bluff him into it, his cunning in holding back Woolley until the Australians' last stand, and his own crusading innings on a broken wicket when the game looked like slipping out of our hands, the great match that marked the climax of his career must have been lost.

The crowd gathered vociferously under the pavilion. Long live Woolley! Long live Hobbs! Above all—long live C. B. Fry! The heroes came to the balcony and bowed their appreciation: but not Charles Fry. The evening newspaper that had explained that he was no real captain, freed from wrapping the luncheon sandwiches, blew about the outfield. Again the cry went up—long live Charles Fry! But the captain who had won them the match, and been booed for his first act in that direction, did not appreciate that it was now his duty to appear on the balcony and graciously receive the cheers of the ignorant. In Greece, in the world he should have adorned, there would have been a parsley crown for this day's work: but it was rather too much to ask him to accept gratefully the plaudits of Kennington. Consider the source.

WORKING MEN'S
COLLEGE
LIBRARY

CHAPTER 5

The Captain is a Critic

THUS ended Charles's cricket career, in the great arena of international conflict. He finished the season head of the averages, as if by old established custom. For a year or two yet, he remained unassailable as a run-getter. In his fiftieth year, with World War I behind him, he was good enough to come out of his tent and show the new generation how Gregory and McDonald should be dispersed about the boundary. If he hadn't knocked up a finger catching an old friend in Warren Bardsley at the end of a double century, he would have been committed to captain England in the later Tests of that calamitous season. As it was, he contented himself with watching Lionel Tennyson, his nominee, gratefully accepted by authorities finally attentive to his nod or beck, anticipate the Dunkirk spirit in a rearguard action at Leeds.

I am glad he ended on the note of victory. And I would have you observe that Charles Fry prospered, as the happy English captains have always prospered—F. S. Jackson, the chirpy Warner, the gusty Chapman (though Jardine was more grim than gay). If you played under Archie MacLaren, you entered upon every game bowed down with the Herculean labour of a cricket match against Australia: you went as in a trance to your high destiny of doom. But if you played under Jackson, when things got bad your captain twirled his moustache and took the ball and bowled balls that didn't quite bounce twice, and the great guns of Australia roared out and were spiked.

And if you played under Charles Fry, all the blood and sweat and tears had been the diet of your captain's mind before you got the telegram asking you to report for duty. As soon as you stepped on to the field, you were there to enjoy a game, fiercely contested but always happy enough with all the hard bargaining left to the brain that had overshadowed Simon and F. E. Smith in the examination rooms at Wadham. You played your best, because your captain knew you were one of the best eleven men in England. If you failed it was a fluke, and everybody would look forward to seeing you next time the wickets were pitched.

The light-hearted captains of England (who sometimes had lips as firm-set as Mrs. Battle's when sitting down to a rubber of whist) were not the ones who suffered the flank to be crumpled or the line to be breached in the blazing heart of battle.

Looking back across the years to the heroes of his own day and contrasting them with the modern champions gives Charles a chance of which he fails to avail himself: the chance of finding that the game he helped to shape has deteriorated out of recognition. The monocle will go up, but there will be no audible pronouncement of anathema when defensive batsmen settle down to a task that makes chess by correspondence look exciting. There will come no word that in the old days a batsman had to make a score by playing strokes at balls off which he could very easily get out: not by sitting dreamily on the splice for five balls of an over, and scoring safely off the only one without length or subtlety from the pitch. What sort of scores would the old timers have run up if it had been understood that *that* was the way you set about the game? Understood, too, that a century wasn't, in most cases, the sensible limit to an innings?

Why, the only modern batsman in England with the technical equipment to play the game as the masters of his generation had to play it, was Walter Hammond. Walter appealed to Charles as having inherited the mantle of Trumper and MacLaren: Hammond—not Bradman, nor Sutcliffe, nor Headley, nor even McCabe. He swept aside my suggestion that this master, disdaining strokes between long-leg and the bowler, could only be rated as two-thirds of a great batsman. He declared that Hammond knew well that strokes on the on-side were blueprinted by modern bowling strategy to contain all the traps, snares and stratagems in the game. He therefore, if necessary, waltzed backwards towards square leg—and unleashed his majestic cover-drive.

If you remember how Hammond treated the Australian bowlers who packed the field against his off-side strokes during Chapman's tour, you will see the force of Charles Fry's argument. Then, on occasion, the leg-side pickets from Adelaide to Brisbane rang with the noise of his boundaries, like so many well-pounded xylophones.

35

Just as Hammond scorned to operate, by preference, on the leg-side, so Charles himself, against the bowlers of his day, more often than not forswore the off-side like one who has promised his father to keep away from the weaknesses of the flesh until he reaches maturity.

CHAPTER 6

Enemies can be Fun

WALTER HAMMOND has not always been appreciated; and neither was Charles Fry. Mark you, of course, he chose to madden the unco' sportsmanlike with the greatest deliberation. For instance, there was the noble walrus in the front of the pavilion who greeted him on his return from a two-hour century at Lord's with a heartily puffed out, 'Fine innings, sir! Deuced fine innings.' Charles genially responded, 'Did you think so? Surely not? Why, I missed two balls.' From that moment onwards there was one more member of the Old Guard who glared furiously whenever Charles Fry's name was mentioned.

I am sure Charles was glad to be unpopular in such circles. He always had a horror of those who assumed that cricket has an ethical basis and is fair game for the sanctimonious. Even Gerry Weigall earned reproof on this score. I remember an evening at *The George* at Grantham during the first Test Match against Bradman's team in '37. We were a happy party, the only shadow being the absence of E. V. Lucas, near his end in London. Charles had known Lucas even before they sat together at a City dinner, when an admirer of the on-drive had appeared after the brandy to offer a gold ring which once had belonged to Elizabeth Fry to her renowned descendent. 'But I'm *not* related to Elizabeth Fry,' Charles had admitted. 'But I am,' said Lucas, pocketing the ring. Now in Lucas's place sat Sir Dennison Ross, ready to talk the stars out of the sky on any subject from bi-metallism to Schopenhauer, and in any language from Mandarin to colloquial Urdu. A respectful, invariably interested and sometimes comprehending audience was made up by Sir C. Aubrey Smith, Gerry Weigall and myself. In no time the talk turned metaphysical and took wings. If Einstein had dropped in to join us no doubt he would have interjected an occasional comment, but without him we fell back on silent admiration for the glimpses we got of that conversation sparkling above the mountains of the moon or zooming beyond suns that light up other universes. I say 'we fell back on silent admiration': in fact one of us just fell back, and fell asleep. At ten minutes to two, when the question of immortality was being debated against that kink in space which seemed to suggest that eternity has its limits, Gerry Weigall stirred, rubbed his eyes and rejoined us. 'That's it, Charles. That's what it all boils down to—playing with a straight bat.'

I think Charles has always admired those who play with a cross bat because they knock the sanctimoniousness out of cricket. He has never admitted that the conventional idolatry bestowed on the game is deserved. When the rest of the world agrees to consider that half the scoring strokes a batsman is heir to are to be attributed to the great mystique of wrist-work, Charles genteelly guffaws. He produces all the shots attributed to the steel-sprung wrists of any old master, and he produces them by divine right of his hands. He sends the ball in a humming arc round first slip's legs—and the stroke is accomplished by dint of a curious technique which he names the 'wringing the towel motion'. Anyone, he will explain, can wring out a towel: therefore everyone can hit Lindwall through the slips for four. For my part, I have never doubted my ability to hit Lindwall through the slips whenever fortunate enough to touch him with the edge of my bat; but I could not wring a towel if my life depended on it.

But with Charles, consideration of every batting problem takes place in the light of an applied knowledge of the higher geometry. Thus, in his early days, Edrich was not to his taste because, when making a cover-drive, his arms and torso would lend their weight in one direction, while the rest of him fell away towards the rear elevation. The result was a stroke that looked both ways at once, and was liable to fail for lack of a strategic reserve flowing forward against the enemy at the moment of contact.

There was never a time when Charles was not prepared to

show anyone with so much as a tepid interest in the mechanics of athleticism, the most complicated manoeuvre that would upgrade his game by a fraction of a degree. I remember entering a Tasmanian hotel in '37 to find him lying at full length in the foyer, demonstrating to Stanley Worthington that it was possible by a series of catalyptic jerks to reach a catch in the slips even after one had measured one's length on the ground.

But he always had a tenderness for Worthington, and when Australians were making derisive noises about the feebleness of Allen's batting strength, would darkly murmur that one day Stanley (he would have gone to the stake rather than call him Stan) would surprise them all by hitting a ring-tailed boomer of a double century in a Test Match. Alas, it was not to be. Stanley was pursued by injury and ill-health and, after a lamentable start, his opportunity of revealing his true form to Australian agnostics was restricted to the Fifth Test. In the first innings he attacked the bowling like a whirlwind. In three overs he helped Barnett to spreadeagle Nash and McCormick to the tune of 33 runs. He was almost half-way to his century when, in slashing a boundary off Fleetwood-Smith through the bemused leg field, he overbalanced, and after the sort of sword-dance which would have won a prize at a Highland Games, dislodged a teetering bail.

That evening Charles and Neville Cardus talked over the incident with Don Bradman. 'Wasn't it bad luck for Stanley?'

'Bad luck? Why?'

'Well, because the poor chap had been injured or out of the game for half the tour. And then, when at last he gets a chance, this happens. He takes the bowling by the scruff of the neck, and then, quite by accident, goes and knocks off a bail when he's on top of the world. Can you imagine worse luck than that?'

'Worse luck?'

'Yes. Can you imagine worse luck than that?'

'It's not *bad luck* at all,' said Bradman. '*A batsman isn't supposed to knock off a bail.*'

Charles Fry raised his monocle. The Don's little nose remained high in the air.

WORKING MEN'S
COLLEGE
LIBRARY

CHAPTER 7

The Moderns through a Monocle

THIS tilting against the Australians, and the Australians'
attitude to games, has been a major mission in Charles's later
years. In his youth the conflict—the cause for conflict—didn't
exist. Joe Darling was a jovial Squire Western from Tasmania,
who, when Charles at last visited Australia, took him kangaroo
shooting at midnight in a flood-lit lorry rather as Ranji had
taken him panther shooting by carbide arc-light in a Nawanagar
kotah. There was no real difference between our fellows and Joe
Darling's fellows. You played cricket with Joe Darling and his
team as you played against your neighbouring village, or your
rival county. True, one or two of them (McLeod for instance),
had an idea that they were a great deal more important than
their instrinsic skill warranted their believing; but then Dick
Lilley always gave himself the airs of a Moltke if anyone asked
for his advice on strategy in the middle.

But, with the passing of time, a new type of Australian grew
up. When little Clem Hill first came to England in 1896 he was
almost a freak. Australians were—it was well known—giants;
wasn't their nickname the Cornstalks? Forty years later when
Charles first watched the race play cricket on its own midden,
those sawn-off shot-guns, Bradman, McCabe, Badcock, Hassett
and Gregory, who could almost have adorned a Bantam
Battalion of a cockney regiment, were regulation size. And, of
course, as it grew smaller, the race grew more self-confident.

When he was too old to tackle them on the field, Charles set
about tackling their native self-confidence in a full-scale counter-
propaganda campaign. He observed that when Australian
teams reached England, the press set up the chorus that each
was a side of world-beaters such as had never before graced this
island. The *Miserere* was pretty well unanimous. Once in a
while some ex-England captain would rally the troops with the
hysterical assurance that he remained an optimist. One turned
with relief from such marrow-freezing comfort to professional

pessimists who explained that Billy Brown was far more formidable than Sutcliffe and that Ebeling completely overshadowed Verity, while Woodfull hadn't been bowled since there were horse-trams in the streets of Melbourne, and Frank Ward was a far more marvellous spin bowler than Mailey and Grimmett had ever dreamed of being.

Charles charged forth against the windmill of this press campaign. He lamented that it should be set up by Fleet Street's fifth column in their determination to assure themselves a story that would keep the Loch Ness monster off the front page all summer. He didn't, frankly, think that Billy Brown was a terrifying portent—there were plenty of players potentially as good in county cricket. If Hans Ebeling had been born in Essex he would never have been considered for an England team. As for Frank Ward—Charles was noisily unimpressed. If you wanted to know just how limited Australia's vision was, you had only to consider the fact that her selectors chose Frank Ward for a tour and left Grimmett behind.

Charles did well enough with Australian cricketers in waging his lone campaign. They appreciated his intentions, and often admitted that in theory he had a right to his opinions. But he had no chance of converting English cricketers to a proper appreciation of their own merits. The rest of the critics had the ear of all our highly suggestible county teams, who got out dutifully for 181 and 147 on plum wickets, because that was what was expected of them in that station of life to which it had pleased God to call them. But McCabe was allowed to arrive in England as a complete colt without a single century to his credit and to sweep through five Test Matches in the mood of Conquistador.

Of course, when the Englishmen arrived in Australia, the local press was quick to seize the opportunity of explaining that there was really nothing very much to be afraid of. *Omne ignotum* for them was by no means *pro magnifico*. Their line was to tell Australian readers just what they wanted to be told, just as the English press did for their customers. Only there was this difference—the Australian reader enjoyed being told that his was God's own country and his cricketers were fit representatives of such a State, while the English drew a mysterious comfort from being assured that all hope could forthwith be abandoned.

40

Of the individual performers Charles admitted, in pre-war days, Bradman, O'Reilly and Grimmett as having a right to be discussed in the same breath with the giants of his own age—these three and no others. He considered that the standard of play (especially among the bowlers) was sinking, not rising. There had never been an attack to compare with the old-timers, Spofforth and Tom Garrett, Giffen and Turner, Boyle and Palmer. Even the giants of his own day, Hugh Trumble, Howell, Monty Noble and Jones, whom Ranji nominated as the most dangerous destroyer of Darling's first team, did not quite measure up to the Old Guard.

As for the side that overwhelmed England in '48, he watched it at work in the early months of the summer and returned to Hamble by no means staggered by its excellence. His major comment, as I remember it, was that the boys of the young brigade had become so proficient as back players that the ideal weapon to use on them in attack was the half-volley. In olden days this ball was banged for four with the sweeping forward stroke. Now it is examined critically all the way down the wicket and finally poked at in a spirit of empirical research. The catch should come to hand, sooner rather than later.

Of the individual performers Charles professed a special admiration for Morris, but believed you could get an l.b.w. dicision against him early in his innings when he indulges a tendency for patrolling in front of his wicket with his bat a little high for safety. I do not think any of the younger members of the side made him downgrade Hutton and Compton as next to the Don in accomplishment.

The bowling did not cause him to revise his opinion that the graph of Australia's attack showed the accelerating decline and fall of which I have spoken. Bill Johnston was very good and worked very hard, but he was not O'Reilly. And I am sure he would have picked Lockwood (always named by him as of a higher caste than Richardson) before all the Lindwalls and Keith Millers you ever saw roll up the flank of an England team.

At that, he holds a lively opinion of our latter-day game, even if he is able to keep it in proportion. When I last asked him what was the best cricket match he ever saw in his life, he found me a new answer in the fourth Victory match between 'England' and 'Australia' at the end of World War II. In glorifying this match he did not say it was just the sort of game Billy Murdoch's black eyes would have glistened over. He said it was such a good game that it might have been contrived and rehearsed by Hollywood. But then he always had a high admiration of Hollywood: it was one of the dreams of his life to settle himself in the town and await recognition as God's gift to producers for the rôle of the fine old English gentleman.

The gifts of the newcomer have always been of interest to him. The bowler who put the brightest glitter into the monocle in the last twenty years was Douglas Wright. The first time Charles saw him bowl he sat up straighter than I ever saw him at any other game, and to the best of my belief he lapsed into total silence for several (alternate) overs on end. What gripped his interest was something new to cricket; a potential bowler of fastish googlies.

The batsman who, in between Wars, took the eye (or the monocle) was no Test Match candidate, but a beardless boy in J. R. Thompson who adorned the Cambridge team and later played, whenever schoolmasters have holidays, for Warwickshire. Charles would, I am sure, have taken a much longer journey to watch this innocent reveal his exquisite charms than he would undertake to scrutinize young Sydney Barnes' handling of any county bowling account, tricked out with an acquisitiveness amounting to usury. He saw Thompson as an echo of the handsome technique of the past, when *noblesse oblige* compelled the off-drive and the square cut to be gloriously flourished at the risk of your very life. He was a batsman with all the airs and graces in his composition: it really didn't matter that the statisticians who chose Test Match teams would never be expected to hear of his existence.

All the same, now and then he did draw the attention of the authorities to conscious merit, holding its hat by the brim in the ante-room. There was the case of Sam Parker, of the Rifle Brigade, who had been a prisoner-of-war since Calais, and who, when he returned to England, home and the War Office, revived in '45 an ambition to be given his chance by Hampshire. With a view to consummating this wish, I took him along to Charles's box in the Clock Tower at Lord's where he sat between Edmund Blunden and James Agate and picked up without resource to any hearing aid, a detailed description, from his host in the next box, of how Weigall of Cambridge had won the 1892 Varsity match for Oxford by running out F. S. Jackson, C. M. Wells and A. J. L. Hill during his imperturbable innings of 63 not out. There was also some patter about the merits of E. M. Sprot as a billiard-player. After a bewildering lunch interval, Sam Parker returned to afternoon duty at the War Office in a mood of relief. Only one person in the company appeared to have got as far as listening to part of his name—an aged poet who had comfortingly pump-handled his left hand, observing that he was proud to shake the best weapon exploited on a bowler's wicket in the past half-century, which certainly should have been given more than that single chance in '21 to bring about the downfall of an Australian side.

Nevertheless, as a result of pressure from Charles and his friend W. R. Ponting, a week later Sam Parker, while on leave in the North of England, got a telegram of immediate invitation from the Hampshire captain. He accepted by wire, took a cross-country journey by a series of deftly commandeered cars, and arrived to find Hampshire already at the wicket, and heading for a collapse. He had just time to buckle on his pads and get out to the middle to play an innings which saved his side. Charles was pleased when I told him the happy ending to this story. He carefully wrote down Sam's name on his scratch-pad for future reference, but almost immediately used up the sheet of paper as a spill for his pipe.

CHAPTER 8

WORKING MEN'S
COLLEGE
LIBRARY

The Footballer—
Choose Your Own Code

CRICKET—cricket—and again cricket. It always boiled down to cricket in the end. The evenings spent with intimate friends who held Cabinet posts, or wrote the most influential and unreadable leading articles, or unbosomed themselves of golden drama —they all boiled down to cricket gossip in the end. Why was

Lockwood the best of all fast bowlers? And which were the really great captains? Then we should have cheerful talk about the imperturbability of that superb all-rounder, F. S. Jackson, who would bowl a near-wide which a fieldsman whom he had forgotten to move from the leg boundary would conjure into a wicket-taking ball. Or there would be reminiscence about Archie MacLaren, forgotten as a great slip field, though remembered as a magnifico among batsmen.

Always cricket. You would think there had never been any such game as soccer, to say nothing of Rugby football or athletics. And, of course, to say less than nothing about a life-time devoted to running a Training Ship, or many years in Fleet Street, or the time spent in Geneva as a Substitute Delegate for India.

And yet Charles's claims as a figure of major interest in both codes of football and in athletics are important enough to fill in a break in that sempiternal conversation. He himself has always said (or more often than not said) that if he had had an early choice in the matter, he would have made more of a reputation in Rugby than in any other game. He never played till he reached Wadham: when, surviving F. E. Smith's preliminary criticism that he had the air of a fainting schoolgirl when tackling, he made himself into a right wing-three-quarter good enough to be considered for a place in the England team. In one season he played in every match for Oxford, except the match against Cambridge: the reason for his absence being a strained leg muscle in the penultimate game. After term was over, he turned out for Blackheath and shone during a Barbarian tour.

But his most impressive games were probably played for the University. "Plum" Warner has a vivid memory of one such triumph against Blackheath in '94. In those days Oxford played its games in the Parks; and, on this particular winter evening, "Plum" was shaken by the spectacle of an astounded and delirious crowd cheering its hero every yard of the way back to Wadham: a solid phalanx of roaring admirers. Charles had spent the earlier part of the afternoon scoring three tries for Oxford, running round one of the sounder defences in England to ground the goal behind the posts every time.

But rugger was only an embroidery, the real fabric of his

footballing career was the soccer he played for Oxford, the Corinthians and Southampton. His outstanding gift was speed, and he was, of course, designed by nature to be an outside right. But, in his day, nature had no talent scouts in the home counties. Charles became a full back because his house team at Repton was short in that department one afternoon, and the skipper happened to spot him coming out of the changing room. Really, it was a mercy that some such accident did not project him into a lifetime of wicket-keeping.

He played four times against Cambridge, figuring on the winning side in his second and fourth years, losing by three goals to one on a ground like an ice-rink in his third season when he captained what was probably the best side ever put out for Oxford. Three times out of four his partner in the Oxford side was W. J. Oakley, quick enough to win the Inter-Varsity hurdles, and good enough to play full back for England on many occasions. But the most famous player of his day was G. O. Smith, who scored a century against Cambridge when picked as eleventh man for Oxford, and generally voted Tinsley Lindley's rival for the honour of being the most amazing dribbler ever fielded by the Corinthians.

Probably the greatest games of Charles's career (more fiercely contested than the 3–0 victory for England against Ireland in 1901) were those played for the Sheriff of London's Shield. These were contests between the best amateur and the best professional football sides of the year: and probably none was better than the match in the first year of the century, when the Corinthians mudlarked their way through to victory against Aston Villa by two goals to one. The speed of Fry and Oakley at back was the determining factor: indeed, Charles's winged heels won many a game from bewildered opponents. He was quite a new type of full back. The traditional specimen was built on the lines of Tony Galento: a thunderous heavyweight who would barge a forward into a catherine wheel and then, as majestically as Dr. Grimstone himself, punt the ball up-field. Charles beat his opposing forwards with their own weapons. He dispossessed them by sheer speed. He ran rings round them: revealing himself as a sprinter whose football boots happened to be a perfect fit.

Those flyaway feet were also one of the main reasons for

Southampton's success in Southern League football at the turn of the century. Their peak year was 1901–2; one of two years when they reached the Cup Final. They began with two drawn games and then a victory against Tottenham, who had won the Cup from Sheffield United in the previous season. In the second round they beat Liverpool, the League champions, by four goals to one. Then came victories over Bury and Nottingham Forest, and the first of two finals at Crystal Palace against Sheffield United.

The great Yorkshire team (playing in its third final in four years) had one of the most resolute defences then known in football. In goal was the gigantic Foulke; at back were Thickett and Boyle, heroes of the Cup victory over Derby County (with Steve Bloomer at his blooming best) three years earlier. And at left half was the immortal 'Nudger' Needham. Crabtree (Charles's own choice as the greatest footballer of his experience) once said of this unorthodox genius, 'Needham is Needham and he plays his own game. We can all be good players, but we cannot all be wizards, and Ranji and Needham are wizards.' The wizard was too good for Southampton in the re-played final. He engineered the first goal for his side within a minute or two of the kick-off. In the second half Southampton drew level, but just before the end Needham won the match for his side with an oblique shot from far out.

What was football like, forty-eight years ago, when Charles Fry appeared in the Cup Final replay on the Saturday and turned out on the Monday to score 78 for W.G.'s London County team against Surrey? Probably most people feel that whatever it was like it had not the terrific mass appeal it has, for good or bad, today; that teams like the Old Etonians were liable to win the Cup out of sheer class superiority; that Cup Finals were attended by four or five thousand spectators; and that for the most part the game was the preserve of low types on public commons, wearing cloth caps, drain-pipe trousers and shin-guards outside their stockings. Well, when Southampton reached their second Final, it was ten years since an Old Boys' team had been seen in the competition proper, and twenty since the Old Etonians had beaten Blackburn Rovers for the Cup. Professionalism, in spite of the efforts of the F.A., had come to stay; though three seasons were to pass before the first four-figure transfer fee was to be paid by Middlesbrough for Alf Common.

The by no means gently nurtured Corinthian found the professional game in the North and Midlands rather rougher than it need have been. The discovery was by no means confined to amateur players like Fry. Many reputable citizens needed to be convinced that there was any real ethnological difference between the Wild Man from Borneo and the professional footballer. Three years earlier the leading hotel at Birmingham had refused to house the England team to play Scotland until important shareholders from London had reassured the management that their visitors would bear the hall-mark of civilized citizens.

Perhaps no little part of the roughness in the game was due to the founding in '94 of the Southern League (in which Southampton held first place in '02) which undoubtedly sharpened the edged rivalry between clubs of the North and South. The South were out on foray—Tottenham indeed had actually won the Cup in '01, breaking a North-country monopoly which had existed since the Old Etonians' victory in 1882.

As for the amount of public interest the game evoked— well, that drawn Final between Sheffield United and Southampton drew a crowd of 76,914 to the Crystal Palace. At that, there was a good deal of speculation as to whether the Cup Final was quite the spectacle it had been. The year before 110,820 people had watched Tottenham and the United play their first match. Perhaps mass enthusiasm for sport had reached its zenith and was declining, suggested the experts with their fingers on the public's pulse. There were, however, good reasons for the drop in attendance. First of all, interest in the game had been abnormally high because Tottenham was attempting to break the North's stranglehold on the Cup. Secondly, the Ibrox Park disaster in Scotland was still fresh in many people's minds in 1902: during an England-Scotland match a stand collapsed with a loss of twenty-five lives. Thirdly, the country was in the grip of a small-pox scare. Thousands would no more have thought of joining the vast aggregations of people on the Crystal Palace ground than of paying a call on a leper colony.

Finally, there was at this time a crystallizing of feeling against the latter-day fetish of football. As the Football Association's enlightening *Official History of the F.A. Cup* points out, the Nonconformist *British Weekly* and other semi-religious magazines, as well as ministers of all denominations, played their part in checking the flow of public zeal for the game. There were even certain religious conventions which took special pains to prove that football was a pastime of the evil-minded. It took some little time for the public to make up its own mind that even professional football might be watched without incurring eternal damnation. After all, there was the Reverend K. R. G. Hunt playing at right half for the Wolves when they beat elegant Newcastle in the Final: his muscular Christianity was an assurance of respectability.

Charles himself enjoyed the several seasons during which he played for Southampton in the Southern League as much as any football in his career. It was a source of pride to be chosen, together with Robinson who kept goal in both Southampton's Cup Finals, and his own partner at left-back, Molyneaux, for England against Ireland. The Selection Committee's gesture set the seal on the greatness of the defence of the Champions of the Southern League.

CHAPTER 9

The Untutored Athlete

WHATEVER the world's qualifications about the respectability of being an outstanding footballer, nobody disputed your right to excel at athletics on Saturday and take up the collection in church next morning.

You will have gathered that the sporting world Charles Fry adorned was an amateur world. It was about as amateur as the Officers' Mess of a Cavalry Unit setting out to join Buller's army on the wrong side of the Tugela River under the admiring eyes of a gallery of office boys wearing patriotic buttons. In no department was this amateurism more conspicuous than in the athletic arena. Today a world's record is the fruit of years

WORKING MEN'S
COLLEGE
LIBRARY

Entertaining his cadets on the training ship Mercury, his longest and greatest enthusiasm.

of tuition on a campus from which even sweater girls are exorcised by a coach who earns almost as much as a teen-aged film star. The only tuition Charles ever got came from his housemaster at Repton, who once dropped his rolled-up mackintosh over the take-off of the long jump to force the boy to leap not only far but also high.

Nevertheless as an undergraduate Charles equalled a world's long jump record which stood for several years. He never trained to do this jump: he was never taught. He jumped by native wit—and he jumped only when there was a competition to be won. He was smoking a cigar in the dressing-room when the event got under way, and he put this down, pulled off his sweater, ran out to put up the world's record and went back again to his cigar. All his athletic life was run on these lines.

That world's record long jump leap of 23 feet 6½ inches was not the greatest of his career. This was his Inter-Varsity record, put up as a freshman with a cracked wooden take-off board which forced him to jump off the track at least 9 inches behind the starting line. In those days you had to jump off a board which sloped downwards into the pit: over-stepping meant pitching forward and breaking anything from your knee to your neck.

In the Inter-Varsity sports Charles lived up to his reputation for being unpredictable by setting up that record as a freshman, winning the event three years running, and losing by 8½ inches in his last year to the Cambridge first string—a result which cost Oxford the sports.

Then there was the 100 yards dash. He dead-heated for first place at his first appearance; and next year, when the race was won in slower time, he finished last. To this day everyone thinks of him first, last, and all the time as a sprinter. As a matter of fact at Repton he liked sprints best, but after them most enjoyed long races: from five to ten miles. He found a sprint at the end of the longest race, and never knew what it was to be tired. If anybody had suggested to him that he should make himself into a marathon runner he would certainly have fallen in with the idea, even though he never took a practice spin between marathons.

I once asked him how much better he would have been if he had been taught to run and jump. He screwed his monocle into his eye and looked back half a century. His best high jump (he was good enough to be picked against Cambridge) was a modest affair of 5 feet 8½ inches. He thought he could have added two inches here: and in those days that would have been good enough to put him in line for an A.A.A. championship. As a sprinter, he had clocked 10 seconds dead. If they had taught him, he could have cut that down to 9·8. And the great long jump with the help of one of the modern experts who reduce the performance to a simple trigonometrical problem, well within the comprehension of any athlete capable of digesting the binomial theorem, might have been widened by a couple of feet. The adoption of the modern hitch-kick— which Charles defines as a run into the air—should have been worth just about that extra margin to him.

We can (and with Heaven's help we shall) argue for ever as to what the batsmen of the Golden Age would have done to Lindwall or Grimmett. We shall dispute till night falls on us all as to whether for our team against Mars we should pick Millburn or the Corinthian Tinsley Lindley, son-in-law of Burnand of *Punch* who used to ask his dinner guests after the third round of port to pronounce the great footballer's name before joining the ladies. But at first sight the athletic problem might seem to be solved by sheer and mere statistics. Against that is the argument that huge advances have been made in the composition of tracks and in general conditions. And again, against that, one remembers Bradman's comment when the heroes of antiquity and the present age were compared to the advantage of the old-timers: 'The swimmers are lucky; nobody can say that the water has improved.'

I feel myself that if you could bring back W. G. George (who eclipsed the world by running a mile in twenty seconds over four minutes) and set him at his very best to run against Gundar Haegg or the 1948 1,500 metres Olympic winner, the more recent candidate would win by a good many yards. But I also feel that if George and the Olympic Champion were to be born tomorrow and spend their lifetimes under a Dean Cromwell endowed with immortality, it would be extremely unsafe to bet a pound to a dollar against the old-timer.

The point is (and Charles never tires of emphasizing it) that when a new genius arises in a new generation to set up a new athletic standard, all the moderates on the campus suddenly become magnetized to follow closely in his footsteps. Until Charles suddenly leaped 23 feet, all the long jumpers at Oxford were jumping 21 feet like himself. As soon as he promoted himself into the new class, the others automatically added an extra foot to their performance. *Possunt quia posse videntur*, or something of the sort.

CHAPTER 10

Apollo——

WHEN he was not rewriting the history of sport he was living a life which from Oxford onwards was never allowed to be private. To this day it is a theory of his that cricket in the Golden Age had a superior charm because its practitioners disappeared into a mysterious privacy with the last rose of summer. Nobody knew that one member of a county team was a hunt servant, another was a painter of inn-signs, a third was a billiard marker. They all came to life in summer, held the country's interest for five months, and then vanished to be a subject of pleasantly vague speculation during the long winter evenings. Today, so much is written about everybody that only an ignoramus wouldn't know the birthdays, winter occupations, favourite film and chosen hair oil of any cricketer of eminence.

Charles Fry was the first of his kind to have a non-stop spotlight turned on him. What he did was always news. The posters said *Fry Again* or *Fry Fails*. Whichever way it went, from Oxford onwards the public wanted to know all about what had happened to him.

This right to the limelight has continued to be conceded almost to the present day. When he gathered his poets and politicians about him in his box at Lord's, his was the opinion always sought, however far from the playing field the conversation might have roamed.

It was the tribute paid by men of common clay to one who would in Plato's day have been acclaimed as a natural leader of the community. He looks the part. He has the head, not of the olive-crowned champion of the Games, but of the god before whose temple the olive leaves were gathered. He carries his magnificent and legendary body with a noble indifference to the effect produced on those around or below him. He is a leader in the careless English tradition: not one who dominates or gives orders, but one who is a heroic name in the mouths of common men, a glimpse of whom at a distance makes a red-letter day in the lives of his admirers. He is one who was open to every jealous criticism from his peers, but whom his generation accepted as the champion and Admirable Crichton of its day.

It all began at Oxford. One of the stories the world most pertinaciously clings to is of his arrival at Wadham, having beaten F. E. Smith in the scholarship examination. He arrived with £3 in his pocket, took a brilliant First in Mods, an even more brilliant Fourth in Greats, was interviewed by Max Beerbohm on behalf of W. E. Henley for the *New Review*, and was the intimate friend of Lords Simon, Birkenhead and Roche-to-be.

After that, he had his living to earn: life became real, but life never became earnest. Even during his Oxford career the vacations, when most men did their serious reading, had to be given up to tutoring jobs to supplement that £80 scholarship which was all he had to keep his head above water in those far-away days before the Welfare State provided every seeker after knowledge with a lifebelt.

After Oxford came Fleet Street. As soon as an article in the *Windsor Magazine* revealed that there was a young man about who could write instructively and entertainingly on out-of-reach Olympians of the cricket world, the beaten path to his door began to appear. He became the first writer to sign sporting articles in the *Daily Express*. He interpreted sport to the man in the street in a classical style that perched uneasily in the columns of the *Athletic News* like an eagle on its bar in the narrow confines of a cage in the Zoo. He stretched his wings in the *Captain*; he zoomed in the *Chronicle*.

He found himself saddled with launching and editing his own magazine when he called on Sir George Newnes to propound an idea that a new paper should be started for Eustace

Miles to propound the doctrine of muscularity to the British race. Sir George Newnes undoubtedly invented *C. B. Fry's Magazine* to get rid of the other project which was as distasteful to him as to Charles himself, whose ideal of physical culture was a Greek grace, or a Hindu sinuousness, or anything in the world except a bulging bicep. The magazine lasted for ten years before World War I killed it. Charles has often expressed his opinion that the end of World War II was the ideal time for its revival. I am not sure, in the light of recent experience, that he would get the firm of Newnes to give the project their whole-hearted support.

On the side, there were books to be written. In 1899 he edited *The Book of Cricket*, a masterly work which, I am bound to admit, strangely contradicts some of his more recent pronouncements on the development of his own game, and gives credence to the conventional school of thought that he has long rebutted. You will remember, for example, that Charles insists today that he evolved such cricket as he achieved from watching Lionel Palairet play, and from his own inner nature. Yet here, at twenty-seven, we find him dismissing the Palairet influence with a reference to a 'style which he had always despairingly admired'. On the other hand, he states specifically that he 'is aware that from the moment he had the privilege of playing with Kumar Shri Ranjitsinhji he began to improve his game' . . . and 'he learnt such cricket as he knows from K. S. Ranjitsinhji and Mr. F. S. Jackson'.

Well, there you are. *Life Worth Living* or *The Book of Cricket?* K. S. Ranjitsinhji or L. C. H. Palairet? You cannot have it both ways—or can you? My own guess is that having in *The Book of Cricket* described himself as a stiff, ungainly bat who developed sweetness and grace from his association with the Jam Sahib, Charles has ever since regretted opening the door to unimaginative critics who look no further for an explanation of his every scoring shot. Certainly he may have developed a philosophic appreciation of the skills of the game from his close-quarters study of the batsman he venerated above all others. But equally certainly he grafted none of Ranjitsinhji's magic to his own yeoman's technique. I feel that the truth of the matter is that his powers of analysis and engineering skill built up the whole stately edifice of his bats-

53

manship; and then, from time to time, he fatally remembers to give credit to cricketers who delighted him in his formative years, after which the critics leave him with no soul to call his own.

But there were other, less controversial works besides *The Book of Cricket*. There were, for example, certain unacknowledged chapters of Ranji's *Jubilee Book*. The critics, not slow to attribute Charles's prowess to Ranji, never had the perspicacity to mark up to Charles that delectable chapter on strategy in a hypothetical cricket match which for years has been acknowledged as one of the best things Ranji ever wrote.

There was also Charles's only novel, *A Mother's Son*, written in collaboration with his wife, and unfortunately with the zealous help of at least one literary adviser, who must have buzzed about the book, tireless and insubstantial as a mosquito, until his every disfiguring suggestion was adopted. As a result there was, as Charles gloomily admits, 'far too much about God in this book'. On the other hand, rousing descriptions of a steeplechase and a Test Match, both drawn from life in vivid detail, were allowed to survive.

The most important book he wrote before the first World War was, however, his masterly text book on *Batsmanship*. It was to D. R. Jardine what *Sinister Street* was to other young men of the same generation who were more interested in self-analysis than in self-expression. In New Zealand, C. V. Grimmett, not yet looking like an Arthur Rackham gnome, made the work his bed-book. Cricketers next summer will turn to it, like their fathers before them, to learn everything that can be learned from a book about how to make the most of an innings.

CHAPTER 11

WORKING MEN'S
COLLEGE
LIBRARY

—*And* Mercury

OVERLAPPING the journalistic work and the earlier books came what is named in *Life Worth Living* as his life's work. This was the running, for over forty years, of the Training Ship

Mercury on the Hamble river. In 1908, after the death of the founder, Charles Hoare, Charles Fry set himself to see to it that this good ship, which for twenty-three years had trained working-class boys for the Royal Navy and the Merchant Service, should not be forced to close down for lack of funds.

The running of this training ship was at once a romance and a stern battle for existence. *Mercury* took some forty years' service from Charles and his wife, each giving time, energy and judgment ungrudgingly in many honorary capacities from Captain Superintendent downwards. In addition to saving the country the sums of money due to those who usually undertake such jobs, the two of them contributed, up to the outbreak of World War II, about £24,000 towards the running of the establishment.

From the very first they were faced with financial pitched battles. Only when he had raised £2,000 (largely in small donations, chiefly from the racing community) was Charles recognized, as a result of a cross-petition in the High Court, as a responsible person fit to handle the destinies of several hundred boys who were to be made into a *corps d'élite* of both decks of the Royal Navy.

After that, the long tug-of-war with authority was fairly joined. First it was necessary to make authority see that such charitable educational institutions as this should offer the chance of working their passage into the Navy to boys of good behaviour as well as to those who made them a salt-water alternative to an Approved School.

Next there was the question of acquiring a training ship to supplement the existing establishment. The Admiralty offered the loan of several vessels, each of which Charles was quick to accept. Every time a ship was agreed upon, an alternative suggestion was fired in; until at last H.M.S. *President*, a one-time composite sloop, serving as the R.N.R. drill-ship in West India Docks, was put forward and accepted. For six years Commander Fry waited for his ship to come down the Hamble river, past Hamble, just down river from Bursledon where the wreck of a Danish dragon ship can be seen in the mud at low water. In the end an inspection of the ship's company by a First Lord named Winston Churchill caused the dust to fly from the files, and the fine ship, her upper deck appropriately

55

housed-in for training purposes, to be towed into position, astern of *Mercury*.

Nothing was more instructive or entertaining than to pay a visit to what was the chief background to the most important of the several lives Charles has crowded into the past forty years. I paid several in Mrs. Fry's lifetime, and after. I remember watching cricket played on that gem of a ground where Ranji and Duleep made merry on high days and holidays, across which MacLaren's drive rang out, where young Reggie Sinfield, one of Charles's boys who bowled Bradman in the Nottingham Test of '38, first learned the principles of the delectable game, in the intervals of making himself into a credit to an exacting ship's company.

In the big house, that also housed the Fry family, was the shore establishment. I never knew a house with so many clocks; and I never saw a place with so many cricket bats as the passage that led off the Honorary Director's study. This sun-burned beauty was the bat that had scored the double century at Lord's in 1903, the highest innings ever hit for the Gentle-men. The chip missing from this weatherbeaten old-timer was knocked adrift at Hove on an August afternoon in 1904, when Charles scored 229 of his side's 377 against the bowling of Hirst and Haigh, Rhodes and Myers and Ernest Smith. Now and then he would fondle one or another, as an absent-minded man will fondle one or other of his pet dogs. On the walls were drawings that G. F. Watts made of him long ago. At the turn of the staircase was a terra-cotta statue of the belligerent cham-pion, his bat brandished shoulder high.

Not a football photograph was to be seen, but lying under a desk was a large, faded photograph of the record-breaking long jump made as a Freshman at Queen's Club against Cambridge. The track officials are gazing at the airborne jumper, their top hats rising on their bristling heads of hair. Somewhere in the crowd Compton Mackenzie, then a schoolboy at St. Paul's, is watching open-mouthed. I was there when Charles presented him with a framed copy of the remarkable photograph of this event as a memento of the historic event in which both had participated.

Alongside the shore establishment is the chapel, where you would hear as fine and as hearty singing as is to be heard in

Hampshire. It was the tradition of *Mercury* that music is about the most important thing in education. The theatre was another tradition: the Christmas plays were famous.

But perhaps the Hamble river is the most important feature of the landscape. By the time he has lived for a few terms in *Mercury*, every boy is as much a river animal as Rat in *The Wind in the Willows*. He is at home in a yacht with spinnakers out as another boy is at home in an engineering workshop. When they acted the part of hosts to a party of sea scouts, the *Mercury* boys rescued their guests from a watery grave, as soon as these theoretical experts overturned their dinghy, with the perfunctory courtesy and quiet seriousness which the denizens of one element accord to those who attempt to elevate themselves to their company.

My own happiest memories of Hamble are of the river. Here on afternoons when there were no Test Matches to be reduced to pre-digested paragraphs for the benefit of Wimbledon ladies who had never consciously seen a cricket bat, we would repair for refreshment and rehabilitation. Up and down the river Charles and I would glide in one of those heavy rowing boats in which young men on training ships develop what Tartarin called *double muscles*. We would dabble our fingers in the ginger-beer coloured water and wonder why MacLaren had to lead his Test team as if he were *G.O.C., Spartan Expeditionary Force, Thermopylae.* Or we would wonder what would have happened if A. N. Hornby had sent C. T. Studd in a little earlier in that Oval game of 1882, when English cricket died, and its ashes were sent to Australia. Or Charles would inveigh against whatever minor offence the sporting world was committing at the moment—probably the regrettable tendency of the star journalists to write with a view to dazzling Fleet Street rather than to illuminate the minds of the uninstructed reader. And all the time as we dabbled our fingers overboard and debated with gentlemanly heat, Mrs. Fry, in her seventies, rowed us up and down the Hamble river. Only now and then did she pause to correct us on points of fact.

CHAPTER 12

The Man Who Remembered

THERE were other exciting chapters in his life. There were visits to India, service on the Indian delegation to the League of Nations, three almost suicidally close attempts to get into Parliament, and a trip to Australia—far too late—to report the achievement of G. O. Allen's touring team. And then back to England. Back to turning out the daily *C. B. Fry Says* column for the *Standard*—turning out, be it said: not churning out. Everything was grist to that mill. One day there was a skating championship at Wembley, with Cecilia Colledge beating Megan Taylor. Then the lady fencers would be involved in a pool at Bertrand's. Then there was Len Harvey receiving the decision over Jock MacAvoy, to Charles's benevolent mystification. The job suited him. He brought an attentive, educated eye to new subjects, picked out the points that appealed to him and served them piping and spiced to the reader who had never previously had any appetite for such stuff.

The new sports, the games about which he knew nothing, always interested Charles more than the games at which he had spent years of his youth, dazzling the spectators. It was only very rarely that he could be persuaded to watch modern soccer players: one such occasion being when England played and beat the Rest of Europe. Charles's visit was primarily made to make a close-quarters' inspection of Stanley Matthews' sleight-of-foot in action. My major memory of the occasion is that after the game the lift to the directors' box chose to levitate between the earth and the upper element like Mahomet's coffin. One or two ladies showed a disposition to hysteria. The officials caused champagne to be passed through the bars to sustain those of us who had not touched a drop since halftime and Charles wrote *C. B. Fry Says* against the wall of the lift.

He had certain revolutionary ideas about this sort of job, not yet accepted by Fleet Street editors. One was that sports writers wasted their own time and their readers' patience, by perpetually harping on the personalities and activities of football managers. What was of interest, as he saw it, was the players themselves. What was the colour of Macaulay's hair? What shape was Tom Lawton's nose? What porridge had John Millburn?

And, on the side, *Life Worth Living* took shape. Charles wrote it, or more often than not, dictated it to me in his dressing gown and bedroom slippers between breakfast and lunch in his flat at Gloucester Place. He adopted the advice on story-telling given to Alice on what was probably after all the right side of the Looking Glass: he began at the beginning, went on to the end, and then stopped. He never re-cast the book, and he hardly re-wrote a sentence.

His memory skipped back to the days when he crawled through the Orpington scrub with his catapult between his teeth and Fenimore Cooper in his heart. He did not forget Mrs. Humphrey, the only woman he ever really feared, a Roman Matron who made life miserable for a sensitive boy at his first preparatory school. He did not forget Old Cribber, or the Reverend Arthur Forman, his housemaster at Repton, who gave him more advice on sport than anyone else in his career; or Foulke, Sheffield United's gargantuan and rubbery goal-keeper (a Fatty Wynne, not a Billy Bunter), or 'Nudger' Needham; or Sir Pertab Singh of Indore, greatest of all pig-stickers, who once dutifully remained with the ladies after a picnic and when rallied by the most fatuous of his guests as to why he hadn't ridden off with the men, replied wildly, 'Not *liking* pig-sticking, dear lady. Thinking it cruel.'

He remembered the sound of the first cricket stroke he ever heard over the garden wall and the scent of the best tobacco he ever smoked (New Zealand's own Number Three Bulldog Toasted Navy Cut), and the taste of the wine-cool air of the Karoo, not far from where he played his first serious cricket in the intervals of calling on President Kruger in Pretoria and being chased by ostriches, by kind permission of Sammy Woods. He remembered the face of the little Nawanagar peasant who, when Ranjitsinhji had driven a panther into its lair, sat on the entrance so that it shouldn't break for safety. He remembered F. E. Smith's face when he read the notice on the Wadham notice-board, announcing that he had been awarded the fourth classical scholarship, and Charles Fry the first.

The result was an autobiography in the round: more than a picture of its author—a glimpse or a touch of the living man in three dimensions. It gave to the world all he had done, all he had seen, much of what he enjoyed of the fun of the fair. In appreciating these things, you became a friend, though not, I think, an intimate, of the man who told the story.

CHAPTER 13

The Scholar

WHEN THE story is read and considered, what conclusion do you reach about its hero? On the surface his is, as I see it, a threefold personality. He is scholar, man of action, and grandee.

As a scholar, his interests are severely classical. Once when he was winning his colours in the Brains Trust, an optimistic mother wrote to him to say that her boy had spent in the Army what should have been his years at the University, and could her favourite omniscient send a list of the Hundred Best Books in English to give the lad a foundation of culture? He passed the letter to me, and, being in the War Office, I was able to devote a certain amount of leisure to the task of compiling a heavily conventional schedule, unenlivened by a single touch of imagination. Charles did me the honour of reading it through with proprietorial vanity before posting it on. He remarked that of my hundred classics, he had read precisely one: *Pickwick Papers*. He had not enjoyed it. I am by no means sure he has read as many plays of Shakespeare as schoolboys digest for the Higher Certificate. In fact, the only play I can vouch for is *The Merchant of Venice* in which he once played the Prince of Morocco, cutting the words 'Oh Hell' from the line he uttered on opening the wrong casket, on the grounds that they might be Shakespeare, but they would certainly make him giggle.

Yes, the English classics passed him by. On the other hand I once took him to a learned diplomat's lecture on a textbook on

Government written by a Pole in Latin during the last years of Elizabeth's reign. Charles discussed the book knowledgeably, to the bafflement of the lecturer who finally exclaimed, 'But there are only two copies of this work in existence.'

'Of course,' replied Charles airily, 'I read the one in the Bodleian.'

He read it, I am sure, with more interest than he ever showed in any book published in the last couple of decades. Conning Greek and Latin authors has been one of his chief intellectual occupations in recent years. Talking to (rather than with) intelligent companions, has been the other. If there were no classics to read or clever people to be talked to, he would fall back on such amusements as translating segments of the English hymnal into Greek or Latin verse. It pleased him far more than making centuries when *The Times* printed these works.

WORKING MEN'S
COLLEGE
LIBRARY

CHAPTER 14

The Man of Action

SECONDLY, the man of action. Secondly, because I feel that this is the secondary and not the primary Charles Fry, in his own estimation. It was only as an exercise of a by-product of his personality that he happened to outjump and outbat the world. He wanted to be a poet; he was a scholar. He would never have eclipsed all other athletes if he hadn't happened to be interested in rhythm, physical rhythm as well as the rhythm of the singers and the painters. He applied this interest, amounting to an integrated technique, to the games the world put into the Christmas stocking of his boyhood. The result was that he surpassed all comers. To him, at least, it was incidental that he scored centuries. A small innings of beautiful strokes off beautiful bowling was much more to his taste than a line in the record book. As a sportsman he was an engineer first, with aspirations towards the technical felicity of the artist.

That was, as I think, how he saw it. The world saw it otherwise. The record in aggregate was the greatest known in this line of endeavour. Nobody else could approach such a string of honours: captain of England at cricket; an England footballer; a Blackheath and Barbarian Rugby player, kept out of the Oxford side by accident; a world record holder in the long jump; and a University sprinter and high jumper.

When you consider the great all-rounders, you find yourself wondering who has a right to second place; there is never any doubt in your mind as to who is the champion.

Perhaps *Proxime accessit* would be Max Woosnam, captain of England at football and lawn tennis, and twelfth man for Cambridge at cricket. Or again, you might nominate Denis Compton, who would undoubtedly have been a full-scale football international but for the fact that no caps were given during the war years. He is on the list of great cricketers who were footballers too, which includes Ducat, Hendren and Hardinge.

For the record, there are other interesting claimants. There is 'Tuppy' Owen-Smith, who played marvellous cricket for South Africa and superb Rugby for England. There is R. H. Bettington, whom H. V. Horden taught to bowl the googly which carried him into the Gentleman's side, who was one of the majestic Rugby forwards gracing Oxford's team in the twenties, and who won the Australian Amateur Golf Championship in 1932. There is 'Snowy' Baker, runner-up in the Olympic boxing of 1908, who played Rugby for Australia at seventeen, was a champion swimmer, an excellent sprinter and miler, and a notable rider and polo player. There is Jack Davies, who will never live down his reputation of having bowled Bradman for a duck when an undergraduate at Cambridge; but who adds to that a notable record as Rugby three-quarter, and is best of all at fives. There is Dr. Kevin O'Flannagan, good enough for Ireland at both Soccer and Rugby, a national sprint and long-jump champion, first-class at hurling, admirable at lawn tennis. There is Gander Dower, the best ball-game player of his generation, with the wrong technique for every game, possibly due to the fact that he was a natural left-hander, persuaded by a nurse (who did not think such a looking-glass attribute quite nice) to turn himself inside out and present himself as a right-hander for the sake of propriety. Or perhaps you would pick Major H. L. Fleming, an infant prodigy of the 'eighties, who held the Public Schools' record for throwing the cricket ball, was invited to play for Scotland at Rugby, played for Scotland at cricket, was lawn tennis champion of India and Ireland, played for Burma at polo, won the Amateur Billiards Championship at his first attempt, and was a formidable competitor in the Amateur Golf Championship.

Every one of them a great all-rounder.

But none of them a C. B. Fry.

For one thing, all of them could do something, but what was there that you could be sure Charles couldn't do? What was there you could be sure he wouldn't attempt? Since World War II ended, I have known him make up his mind to become a coal-miner, in the interests of pushing a recruiting campaign. He set about trying to get a billet, but the authorities were not broadminded enough to perceive that such an athletic feat would have been, at over seventy, the final, crowning achievement for our great all-rounder. It was with good reason that, as Agate quoted in *Ego*, I was puzzled when he announced at dinner a year or two ago that he was sick and tired of cricket and proposed to interest himself hereafter in racing. He would attach himself to a training stable, learn all about it, and then set up on his own—and he was quite sure he would make a resounding success of it.

'What as?' I asked. 'Trainer—jockey—or horse?'

CHAPTER 15

The Essential Charles

FINALLY, there is Charles the grandee. Here he reaches the crown and consummation of his career. He is the host, not the guest: the hero, not the audience. Whoever else is in the presence, the spotlight is sure to be on him. He is the natural leader, the born exemplar—this jovial figure whom the world insists on looking up to. In a properly regulated world he should have been given (not paid) £30,000 a year to cut a dash for the good of the country. Instead, he had to earn a living to pay his way: to pay for the privilege of associating with the gilt-edged amateurs of his day whom he never allowed to exhibit a fraction of the hospitable impulses he permitted himself. I wish I had seen him in intimate association with the Rajahs. It would have been interesting to see who was the most regal and the most carelessly generous figure in the party.

Well, he paid his way. And for some thirty years he has been the greatest figure in the world of cricket; but he has never been elected to the Committee of the M.C.C. He surveys this deprivation through his monocle, in a mood of dignified amusement.

What is the hall-mark of the Grandee? It is not, I think, magnificence. That is a cheap trick which even millionaires can manage. But the refusal to be touched by backbiting or injury, the ability to hold oneself calmly and cheerfully above the ruck, that is not so easy. That is his gift. Enemies can be jealous of him. The unsuccessful can deride him. He himself remains generous, never stooping to repay criticism in kind. I do not suppose his oldest and most intimate friends ever heard him say a bitter or even an unkind thing about anyone; not even about the fools who gather as camp followers in the wake of every great sportsman.

Ranji called him Carlo; and if you liked to call him Carlo Khan you would not be unjust to the splendour of his personality, seen in the sadly common light of day. But he himself chose as the sub-title of his autobiography, *Some Phases of an Englishman*. The operative word is the last. In the brilliant noon of our history, when that word meant most, it would have been the aptest word of all to sum up Charles Fry.

WORKING MEN'S COLLEGE
LIBRARY

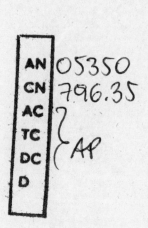

AN
CN
AC
TC
DC
D

05350
796.35

{ AP

WORKING MEN'S
COLLEGE
LIBRARY